To Charlie—An extraordinary young man whose amazing resilience inspires me to keep moving forward and reminds me how fortunate I am.

Acknowledgments

I owe a gargantuan "thank you" to over 300 people around the globe who have had a part in bringing this book and the ideas herein to life. You will find each and every one of them (developers, moms, dads, writers, bloggers, and reporters) within the pages of this book. A huge "gracias" to Gary who kept himself busy painting the house while I spent endless hours staring down the computer screen and tapping at the keyboard. My teenagers who attempted to stay out of my hair, thanks for trying. And of course, thank you mom, my biggest cheerleader.

Big-time "thanks" also to my colleagues; Kelley Yanes, Gina Banks, Harumi Kato, Thomas Todd, Jim Elliott and America Gonzales who encouraged me, covered for me, and gave valuable information and insights to support my research.

One final heartfelt "thank you" goes to Kelly Gilpin, Michelle Vardeman, and the folks at Future Horizons for giving me the chance to share this information with you, the august reader.

~ Lois Jean Brady

Table of Contents

Foreword

With such high levels of interest in this topic, it is crucial for books like this one to be written. I was honored and excited when Lois asked me to contribute the Foreword. Let me share with you a bit about how I became involved with this tremendous movement towards ubiquitous educational technology for people with autism.

Being the co-creator of the original *Proloquo2Go* AAC App for the iOS has taught me about the sheer strength of people coming together with a goal of making a difference. I had a vision and I acted on it, collaborating along the way in order to try to make a difference. With the success of *Proloquo2Go* and my credentials as an AAC specialist and an assistive technology specialist, I have been fortunate to have great opportunities to present and teach in the U.S. and internationally on the topic of new mobile technologies for individuals with disabilities. It has been a phenomenal experience teaching and connecting with parents and teachers who seem so excited that they could burst.

I will always remember the intense feelings I had when I first started pitching my idea to build an augmentative and alternative communication (AAC) application for the iPhone and iPod touch (the iPad did not yet exist as a product). The scene was a national conference and I met with a few "big" companies and a few independent software developers who all said "no" or that it couldn't be done (including some with whom I would later collaborate). One conversation in particular will always stick with me. In a meeting focused on pitching my idea to one of those larger companies, I was posed the question, "But what's so special about the iPhone, why is it any different than the PDA-based communication devices out there now?" Being a bit sheepish about the question, as it was one of my first big meetings in the field, I hesitantly answered with something about how it was Apple and was cooler. Little did I know that less than a year later I would be able to come back to one of those developers with a proposition to collaborate, and then less than a year after that, the vision would become a reality.

David Niemeijer, of Assistiveware, and I built what would become *Proloquo2Go* and it was officially released to the public in April 2009 (Sennott and Bowker, 2009). It came about because the community believed in it and because David and I were able to come together with complementary skills at the right place and the right time.

The first major story about *Proloquo2Go* (and about the iPhone and autism for that matter) was in USA Today. It was about a young boy with autism who was able for the first time to tell his mom that he loved Chinese food. My fiancé would later remind me about how clearly this showed how simple, random things you would be hard-pressed to know about someone are revealed when there is a communication system that works.

From there things really took off quickly, with features by ABC News, IEEE, and Good Morning America about the users of *Proloquo2Go*. Then the dam broke. A mom with ALS and her young son with Down syndrome, both *Proloquo2Go* users, were featured on the front page of the New York Times in a full color photograph. There was public outrage that the Centers for Medicare and Medicaid Services (CMS) would readily purchase devices and equipment at the near $7,000 funding level (each), but not provide these two individuals with iPod touches for a few hundred dollars. The world was talking about Augmentative and Alternative Communication.

It started to feel like a bit of a revolution was happening. We were getting streams of emails from people saying that for the first time, their son or daughter was communicating. At the peak, *Proloquo2Go* hit number four in the top-grossing section of the Apple iTunes Store. Literally, thousands of people were getting access to communication tools.

Sometimes I would be moved to tears upon hearing these stories or seeing the analytics of the numbers of people served. At one point, my father shared with me a quote by Buckminster Fuller about how to create change: "You never change things by fighting the existing reality. To change something, build a new model that makes the existing model obsolete." That being said, educational software was not created with the Apple iPhone, iPod touch, and iPad. In fact, there is a rich tradition of high quality educational software. Yet, what the iOS devices and platform have done is make educational software more personal. It is exciting to be a part of this shift.

At this moment in time, we can see that technology is changing our lives and that change is exponential (Kurzweil, 1999, Moore, 1998). New mobile technologies for people with autism are creating new opportunities at an exponential rate. The message is that we can create tools that can make profound differences in the trajectory of people's lives and in education in general. If we try, we can harness that exponential innovation. Yet, the diffusion of innovation must proceed successfully: early adopters are charged with this sharing of the good news. We must share current knowledge about what is available, along with the benefits and limitations of these new tools. That is why this book is so important.

The first time I saw Lois Jean Brady was in a photograph of her, Temple Grandin, and Buttercup, Lois's pot-bellied therapy pig. Yes, Lois has a therapy pig, as well as a dog, and a horse too! I proceeded to read about how she thoughtfully used animal-assisted therapy as a way to make speech pathology sessions motivating and dynamic. She certainly seemed to be out of the box, in both a refreshing and very relevant way! I looked forward to meeting her in person.

When we first met at the ASHA Convention, we spoke about this book and its importance. We shared our enthusiasm for the newest Apple technologies and for what they were doing to help the individuals with disabilities whom we serve. We spoke about the need for basic information and for the knowledge of a select group of early adopters to be communicated to a broader audience. Clearly, Lois was driven to educate parents and teachers about this topic, which she herself was so passionate about. What a gift.

Lois has taken an important leap in writing this book, providing a much-needed primer for considering the newest, mobile, educational technologies from Apple. "Zach's a Mac" poignantly reveals the experience of one family finding a way to communicate with each other—something that neurotypical families take for granted. Lois's focus on individual student needs is a particularly relevant message and essential to the responsible introduction of educational technologies. She says, "Have a clear focus on the individual's needs. Educators and caregivers should clearly understand and commit to common goals based on the individual's unique needs and abilities." With all of the enthusiasm about new mobile technologies, there is danger that we can lose sight of the need to custom tailor educational solutions for each individual. The knowledge shared in this book can help combat the temptation to disregard thoughtful, individualized solutions by providing information about features, benefits, and limitations.

For parents, teachers, and therapists, it is important to understand what the individual apps can and cannot do, and to be able to carefully consider features relevant to individual needs. From communication to literacy, recreation, and accessories, *Apps for Autism* provides a wealth of useful information to read and reference.

During Steve Jobs's recent keynote regarding the announcement of the iPad 2, a video featured how the iPad is helping individuals with autism in a myriad of ways. A huge audience saw it, representing just how big this technological innovation has become. The time is now to embrace this innovation and welcome the potential that these tools offer. We all can learn from Lois's insight and generous sharing of this much-needed knowledge.

Samuel Sennott

The Pennsylvania State University

State College, PA

References

Kurzweil, R. *The Age of Spiritual Machines: When Computers Exceed Human Intelligence.* New York, New York: Penguin Books, 1999.

Moore, G. "Cramming More Components onto Integrated Circuits." *Proceedings of the IEEE.* 1998; 8:82-85.

Sennott, S., & Bowker, A. "Autism, AAC, and *Proloquo2Go.*" *Perspectives on Augmentative and Alternative Communication.* 2009; 18:137-145.

Introduction _____

In August 2010, Apple Hot News noticed a "quiet revolution" taking place in the autism community focused on using the iPad for teaching communication and social skills to children with autism.

While enjoying dinner with my husband at a local restaurant, a family entered and was seated at a table close to ours. It did not take long to notice that the youngest daughter had autism. After a few minutes, she began rocking, vocalizing, and stacking the menus. Just when it seemed that she was on sensory overload, her dad reached into his pocket and pulled out his iPhone. They began playing a turn-taking game. Both were entertained and interacting the entire time. No words were spoken, just the passing of the iPhone. I do not know what app they were enjoying, or even if it were educational (my first thought), but they did have a nice family dinner at a fancy restaurant. Wow, now there's a use for a smart phone that I did not think about. Way to go, Dad!

Thank you, Apple! Finally, devices that support communication, scheduling, academics, social interactions, video modeling, and leisure time are wrapped up in hand-held, super-cool packages. Individuals who cannot use a mouse or keyboard can use the iPad, iPhone, and iPod touch because there is no disconnect between the screen and the keyboard/mouse. Parents are thrilled and therapists are getting goals met and exceeded. I have heard and read countless stories of children taking their parents' iPhones and just intuitively using the apps. iPhones, iPod touches, and now iPads are used to entertain, communicate, and educate students and learners of all ages and levels. There is no flicker or high-pitched noise. According to Dr. Temple Grandin, some kids are sensitive to the flicker of traditional screens and do much better with laptops because the flat panel displays don't flicker. Also, many kids are sensitive to high-pitched noises. I am a speech-language pathologist and have worked in the field for more than 20 years. I have spent years trying to make traditional devices fit into the world of autism. Ultimately, they end up as very expensive door stops. USA Today's Greg Toppo calls traditional "text-to-speech" devices "huge, heavy, and expensive."

Alas, I have heard of one negative comment regarding the use of iPads, iPhones, and iPod touches. The person comments, "Using an iPhone or owning one puts them at risk of theft. The clunky ole Augmentative Communication device is not something the neighborhood thugs are going to pinch but the temptation changes when it's an iPhone hooked onto the wheelchair or whatever."

Let me answer this. Of course nobody wants to steal an old ACD, because nobody wants one. Not even the individuals who have to lug them around want them. They are heavy, cumbersome, limited in their use, and tell the world, "I am different."

A thief would have to steal 16 iPads, 35 iPod touches, or 24 iPhones to equal the cost of one Dynavox, Springboard, or Say-it-Sam (approx $8,000). I'll take my chances.

I wrote this book to help parents, educators, therapists, and individuals with disabilities navigate through the mountain of apps and gadgets available. I encourage everyone to explore the apps and see what these "magical" devices can do. Many are free or under $2.00. I have been using the iPod touch for over three years and more recently the iPad. My students have had tremendous success and not one inappropriate use of the devices has occurred. They will even carry them without protest. The apps are updated periodically by the developers for free. So I encourage every individual to please explore and use apps: communicate, calculate, read, socialize, have fun, and *enjoy dinner*.

In the News

"Zach's a Mac"

—by Nathan Charlan

We got Zachary an iPad. To some, this may seem like a rash, expensive purchase of a trendy, fashionable gadget (and a ridiculous one at that) for a child who is three and a half years old. I can understand how some might make that interpretation. But I care not. Because Zach's a Mac, and he's using his apps to educate and communicate.

I'll admit plainly that I bashed the idea of the iPad when it was announced. I have a laptop, I have an iPod, why would anyone need an iPad? Lame. Stupid. Another silly gadget.

About eight weeks ago, however, a tech-savvy, gear-crazed friend of mine came over for dinner and brought his brand new iPad. (He may have stood in line for hours to be one of the first in Colorado to own one.) He extolled the virtues of this fine new piece of gadgetry and how his life was very much improved because of it. I didn't buy into it—it still wasn't enticing for me. It looked cool, but so what?

Then, he quickly downloaded a free "painting/drawing" app and handed the iPad over to Zachary. After careful consideration of what this new "toy" was, he started moving his fingers over the screen, and lighting up in excitement when he saw the correlation between action and result. He was drawing by using only his fingers as the paintbrush and it made a "swish-swish" sound when he did it. Zach was hooked. And this was only a "play" app with painting, not even something educational. Renee and I became intrigued. Could it be that our three-year-old son with Cerebral Palsy, and difficulty controlling his finger and arm movements, could control and manipulate a computer? An iPad? Yes. Because Zach's a Mac.

Around this time, our traditional therapists were urging us to get a communication device. OK, what will that take? Well, the one they recommended was PC-based, cost about $10,000, and would take about six months to receive. When it comes, it's the size of an old 17" vacuum tube-powered television set, and its only capability is strictly as a communication device. Sounds fun, versatile, and easily transportable! Yea!

Somewhere along the line (maybe it was an Internet story, a newsletter, or a listserv comment), someone mentioned that there was a communication app and that they were using it on an iPod touch for their older kids. Research began on my part and I found the app was also available for the iPad. It's called *Proloquo2Go*. Its website says the app "provides a full-featured communication solution for people who have difficulty speaking. It brings natural sounding text-to-speech voices, up-to-date symbols, powerful automatic conjugations, a default vocabulary of over 7,000 items, full expandability, and extreme ease of use." The communication app cost about $179 to download; that's kind of expensive, comparatively speaking, to other apps, but, let's see …

- Lowest model iPad: $500, with the ability to download multiple apps for educational purposes, interactive books, and learning games. Communication app, *Proloquo2Go*: $179. Availability: immediate.

- Therapist-recommended, PC-based communication device: $10,000, with the ability to download viruses. Availability: 6 months or more.

Hmmm … maybe the iPad isn't so stupid after all.

Renee and I talked about it and decided it would be a good purchase for Zachary. It wasn't until we actually got to the Apple store to get more information that we were completely sold—hook, line, and sinker.

The store model had a PBS educational game app called Super Why. Zach loves watching Super Why; it's a cartoon about reading, stories, characters, letters, words, and rhyming. Zach started playing with the app. The on-screen character of one of the Three

Little Pigs asked Zach to spell a word by finding the letters one at a time. He'd ask, "Let's spell the word KEYS. Find the letter K." Three choices of letters spread across the screen. Zach immediately chose K. Then the Little Pig asked, "Find the letter E." Boom. Zach picked E and moved onward for 100% accuracy. He continued playing and LOVED it!

Done. Sold. Zach's a Mac.

After having it now for a few weeks, we've managed to download dozens of free educational apps that help Zachary learn and show us he knows what he's learning. He knows his entire alphabet. He knows all his numbers. He knows his animals, shapes, and colors. And now he's starting to mimic the sounds of animals (he'll choose a Bee in one of his animal apps and make the "Buzzzzz" noise. He's never been able to make animal noises before).

We also downloaded the *Proloquo2Go* and are working on it with him. It can be complicated and multi-dimensional, but just yesterday, he selected this app and hit "I want," "something," "something to eat," "fruit." He then hit every fruit button on there, to which I replied that all we had in the house were strawberries. I helped him scroll down to "strawberries" and had him push it. "Strawberries," it said. I took his hand up to the top to tap it and the device said, "I want something to eat, strawberries." I gave him one right away.

While he may have just "accidentally" gotten to this app and hit buttons at random, he's been exploring it lately, checking out all the things the different buttons say. So any time he does access it, I will listen and do my best to show him he can use it to communicate. It'll be a learning process and he'll need time to poke around and explore all the buttons to know them all. He may not be using it "purposefully" quite yet, but he'll get there. We're working on it with him.

Zach absolutely LOVES his iPad. He knows what it's called; he can navigate through it and select apps, going in and out of them. Just the other night, he was able to turn it on and unlock it all by himself!

For us, anything that will benefit Zach in any way—therapy, education, etc.— is what we as parents want for him. We all want the best for our children. He's truly impressed me with his skills at this sleek, cool computer tablet. One of our therapists even recently commented that Zachary (although still nonverbal) is at his age-appropriate cognitive level!

Zach's a Mac. And we're proud of that.

We're looking forward to his continued progress developmentally and if the iPad, with all its cool downloadable educational apps, can help him in that regard, we are excited to watch.

I do realize there are many negative viewpoints when it comes to getting a child involved with computers at a young age. Well, Zachary's different. He has special needs. He cannot talk, cannot sit on his own, cannot walk, cannot run, cannot play like typical kids. As parents, we work and play with Zach every day, hands-on, more involved physically than parents of typical children who have the abilities to run around, play, and be partially independent. Naysayers of the iPad's usefulness for children can take a walk, because it's useful to Zach, useful to his learning, and useful to his overall development. He can show us how smart he is. He can use it to talk and communicate to us. And that is absolutely invaluable.

About Apps for Autism

How to Use This Book

Definition

What is an app? The word, "app" is short for computer application. Simply put, a computer application, or app, refers to a program that allows the user to accomplish a task. There are more than 425,000 apps available from the iTunes store. Thousands are added each week. I have done my best to search through and find the apps that would be most beneficial to individuals with autism spectrum disorders and other disabilities.

Structure

I have spent over three years using, testing, taking notes, collecting opinions from colleagues, parents, users, and combing through research on the World Wide Web to present the most useful, up-to-date information possible. Apps for Autism is divided into 32 chapters; it was very difficult to decide the appropriate chapter for each app. The FingerPiano, for example, would be equally at home in the Occupational Therapy section or could fit into the Creative Learning or Music sections. In the end, I just went with how my students use it best. I felt strongly enough about several apps to include them in more than one section so that they would not be overlooked; for example, the SmallTalk phonemes app is in the Apraxia chapter. However, it is also an excellent app for articulation, so you will find it in both. I have added personal success stories, articles, insights, and testimonials from colleagues, parents, and myself to demonstrate the endless possibilities. Please remember, everyone on the autism spectrum is different. They will all have a different combination of apps that fit their personal needs, abilities, goals, and interests. Our job is to guide and reinforce, not dictate and insist.

Content _____

Prices are listed for each app. These prices were accurate at the time I bought the app. Developers may change prices and upgrade frequently. Upgrades are usually free. The information is correct at this moment; however, it may change tomorrow.

Throughout Apps for Autism I may use the word iPhone, iPod touch, or iPad; however, in most cases, I really mean all three. Almost all apps can run on the iPhone, iPod touch, and iPad. The iPod touch (versions 1-3) will need an external microphone to record audio on the apps that are customizable. Many times I will just use the word, "iDevice."

I have formatted the app pages with screen shots, logos, websites, prices, some information from the developers themselves, and customer reviews. The developer's information explains the purpose of each app and what he or she wants you to know about it. Customer reviews are collected from personal experience, colleagues, teachers, parents, and users themselves. Last but not least, some apps are available in Lite (free) versions. I wholeheartedly recommend trying the Lite version first. If you do not like it, delete it. No money frittered.

What is iTherapy?

Technology, for the most part, contributes to the betterment of society. In the realm of education, technology has become an integral part of the system. Educators from all over the nation are using technology in their repertoire to enhance classroom learning. Among the many benefits is greater access to education for everyone, but in particular, technological advancements have opened education more than ever to learners with disabilities like autism spectrum disorders.

iTherapy capitalizes on the latest technologies available from Apple like the iPad, iPod touch and the iPhone. At its core, iTherapy refers to the use of an Apple product in combination with an app (computer application) in a therapy environment as a modality to meet goals implemented by an IEP team.

Software (apps) for any of the Apple products is readily available from the app store located within the iTunes website. Currently there are about three hundred thousand apps with more added on a daily basis. You can use these apps individually or combine them to achieve a set goal(s). Whether you are using voice output, building vocabulary, correcting articulation, or strengthening muscle coordination, any of these devices make it easier, more fun, and reinforcing.

In addition, learning goes on long after the therapy session has ended. Unlike other computer-based therapies, students can take their Apple product wherever they go, thus allowing them to engage in learning whenever the opportunity presents itself. Not to mention, their Apple products can hold music and movies. Alas, they too can be cool!

In short, when you combine Apple's hardware with software like *Proloquo2Go* or

First Words: Deluxe, the result is AAC (Augmentative and Alternative Communication) that is powerful, portable, desirable, yet affordable. Set this in a therapy environment with a focus on predetermined goals designed by an IEP team, and you get iTherapy: an effective learning strategy.

Best Practices and Educational Guidelines

In this section I will review strategies, techniques, and guidelines that have been successful in a variety of settings. The term "Best Practices" is used to describe the techniques and strategies that work well in a particular situation or environment. Grover J. Whitehurst talks about best practices as the integration of the professional wisdom of educators and family members with research-based practice. With that in mind, here are a variety of Best Practices and teaching strategies that are relevant for utilizing technology in education.

1. Have a clear focus on the individuals needs. Educators and caregivers should clearly understand and commit to common goals based on the individual's unique needs and abilities.

2. Maintain high standards and expectations for all individuals to succeed. Assume that each and every individual can learn how to use technology in a capacity that is relevant to them. Individuals can achieve great success when standards of performance are made clear, consistent, and all members of the team are dedicated to helping every individual achieve his or her goal.

3. Consider the individual's environments and the skills needed to function in those environments. Home, school, community, etc., present variable challenges. We need to consider what set of skills an individual needs to participate and be productive in each environment. In essence, we should draw upon the entire community to foster student achievement.

4. What are the appropriate tools, gadgets, devices, apps, programs, and accessories that can be effectively accessed by an individual? Consideration must be given to the individual's vision, motor planning, attention, sensory processing, memory, and cognitive ability to provide the most effective tools for success.

5. Use as much prompting and reinforcement as necessary to establish a skill, then decrease prompting and reinforcement systematically to the natural environment.

6. Most individuals take to the iDevice like an eagle takes to the air. However, there is the occasional student who needs a bit of encouragement. Not to worry: simply play a favorite song, movie, or show a favorite character and that individual is "hooked." Once "hooked," slowly introduce challenges and structured activities.

7. Last and perhaps most important, teach turn-taking or you may not get your device back. I have heard one common gripe from many parents and colleagues: "I can't get my device back." "My turn," "Your turn" works extremely well in teaching turn-taking techniques. And always take your turn first, to set a good example. The most challenging students will hand over the device when I announce, "my turn." Time limits and timers also work well as short, task-orientated activities. Good luck, and rest assured, you will eventually get your device back.

Icons

There are three features that have become very important when using an app in the educational setting. I have given each of these features an icon. The icon will appear under the title of the app if the feature is included in that app.

 REPORTS: The email envelope icon lets you know that the end product, data, or message can be emailed directly from the iDevice to parents, teachers, and yourself for review, records, or generalization. This feature also allows educators to keep in touch with families, friends or caregivers, and share accomplishments.

 DATA: The pencil icon represents data collection. Educators can spend much of their time collecting and analyzing data. If an app can do that, GREAT— more time for the students.

 IMAGE SEARCH: The magnifying glass icon lets you know an Internet image search is available with this app. Having the ability to search the Internet for just the right image to represent a concept, person, place, or thing is highly motivating to both students and educators.

Getting Started

Choosing an iDevice ───────────────

DEVICES AT A GLANCE

Features	iPhone*	iPod touch	iPad	iPad 2	iPod touch 4***	iPhone 4
Apps	Yes	Yes	Yes	Yes	Yes	Yes
Music	Yes	Yes	Yes	Yes	Yes	Yes
Movies	Yes	Yes	Yes	Yes	Yes	Yes
Camera	Yes	No	No	Yes	Yes	Yes
Mic	Yes	No	Yes	Yes	Yes	Yes
WiFi	Yes	Yes	Yes	Yes	Yes	Yes
3G	Yes**	No	Yes**	Yes**	No	Yes
Dual Cameras	No	No	No	Yes	Yes	Yes

* iPhone requires a data plan unless the device is bought from a third party.

** 3G requires a data plan with a monthly billing cycle.

*** 4th generation iPod touch

When choosing the most appropriate iDevice there are four important areas to consider:

1. Motor control: Do individuals have adequate motor control to activate a single button without touching others? The iPod touch and iPhone require more precise fine motor control than the iPad. Consequently, if motor control is an issue, consider the iPad.

2. Vision: Both the iPhone and iPod touch have smaller screens than the iPad. Individuals who have challenges with visual acuity and perception may favor the iPad.

3. Camera: The iPhone and the iPod touch 4 let the user take pictures for immediate use with the apps. This feature is super handy when making memory books, story boards, and visual supports on the go (field trip, grocery story, holiday, etc.). I have an old iPhone (with no service plan) that I take on field trips to make memory books and then review on the bus ride home. If having immediate access to pictures is important to you, then the iPhone may be your device.

4. Microphone: The iPhone, iPod touch 4 and iPad all have built-in microphones. Microphones allow the user to customize the audio and interact with many apps. There are many choices for external microphones for the iPod touch 1-3; however, built-in microphones are usually preferred, and never lost.

Additionally, take into account portability. The iPad is much larger than the iPhone and iPod touch and cannot be stuffed into your pocket. Still not sure? Visit your local Apple store or www.apple.com for more information.

Basic iDevice Operations _____

Headphone jack — — Microphone

Sleep/wake

Screen rotation lock

Volume up/down

Home —

Dock connector — — Speaker

The basic buttons and controls are the same on the iPad and iPod touch. The iPhone has a few more external (phone related) controls. Quite frankly, I have never used more than the basics on any of my devices, but there is so much to explore!

To get the most out of your iDevices, please visit the Apple User Guide for each iDevice:

- iPod touch User Guide:

  http://manuals.info.apple.com/en_US/iPod_touch_iOS4_User_Guide.pdf

- iPhone User Guide:

  http://manuals.info.apple.com/en/iPhone_user_guide.pdf

- iPad User Guide:

  http://manuals.info.apple.com/en_US/iPad_User_Guide.pdf

Also available from iTunes is a free eBook (iPad User Guide) that has everything you need to know about your iPad.

Opening an Account

To download iTunes and open an account, follow these easy instructions:

1. Go to www.apple.com/itunes/download, click on **Download Now** and follow directions.

2. After you have downloaded iTunes, choose **Store ➤ Create Account**.

3. Read the Terms and Conditions. If you agree, check box and then click **Continue**.

4. Fill in the information to create an Apple ID.

5. Provide method of payment and billing address. (I used an iTunes gift card to open my account.)

6. You can now begin acquiring apps, music, podcasts, eBooks and movies.

For more information please visit: http://support.apple.com/kb/ht2731

How to Download an App from iTunes _____

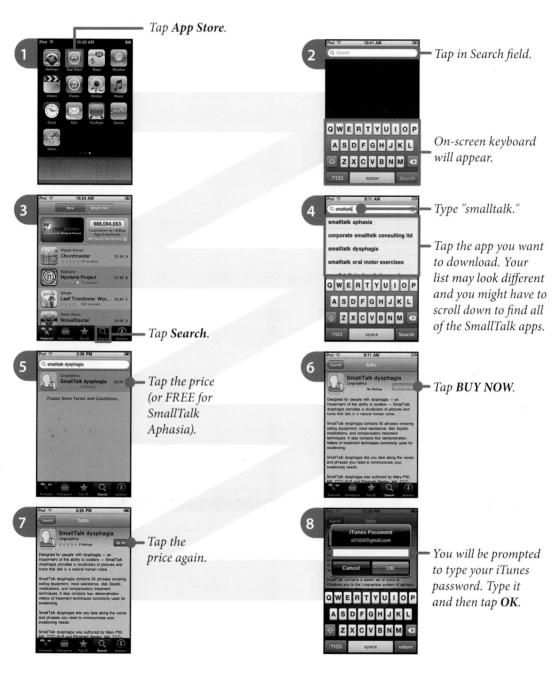

Tap **App Store**.

1

Tap in Search field.

2

On-screen keyboard will appear.

3

Tap **Search**.

Type "smalltalk."

4

smalltalk aphasia
corporate smalltalk consulting ltd
smalltalk dysphagia
smalltalk oral motor exercises

Tap the app you want to download. Your list may look different and you might have to scroll down to find all of the SmallTalk apps.

5

Tap the price (or FREE for SmallTalk Aphasia).

6

Tap **BUY NOW**.

7

Tap the price again.

8

You will be prompted to type your iTunes password. Type it and then tap **OK**.

images provided by  **Lingraphica®**

Getting the Most from an App Purchase Page

Take a moment to get to know this page and make the most of the information available.

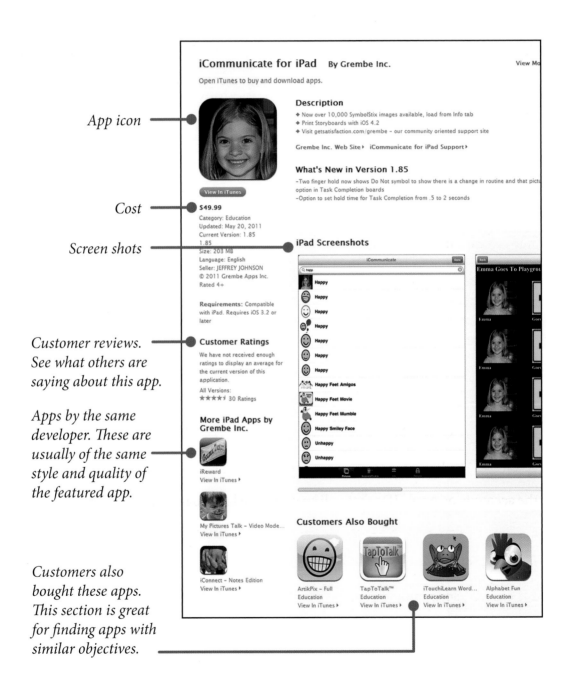

App icon

Cost

Screen shots

Customer reviews. See what others are saying about this app.

Apps by the same developer. These are usually of the same style and quality of the featured app.

Customers also bought these apps. This section is great for finding apps with similar objectives.

Volume Purchase Program _____

In August 2010 Apple launched its Volume Purchase Program (VPP) for iTunes and the App Store. The program allows qualified educational institutions to purchase iOS Apps in volume at a discounted price and distribute those apps to end users. The VPP allows app developers to offer a discount of 50% for the purchase of 20 apps or more. Follow this link to search educational apps that are available for a discount: http://volume.itunes.apple.com/us/store

There are three main characters in the VPP program:

1. Authorized Purchaser: The Authorized Purchaser is often the purchasing agent at an institution. This person provides vouchers to the Program Facilitator(s) in denominations of $100, $500, $1,000, $5,000 and $10,000 to match, as closely as possible the value of the requested apps. Volume Voucher(s) take about 3-5 business days to be received via snail mail. Once received, the Program Purchaser forwards the Vouchers to the Program Facilitator.

2. Program Manager: This person is responsible for managing Program Facilitator accounts. The Program Manager will provide the necessary information related to the accounts or Apple IDs that will be designated at Program Facilitators. Once these accounts are provided to Apple via the Program Manager portal, the Program Facilitator will be able to access the volume purchase site, redeem vouchers and purchase application redemption codes.

3. Program Facilitator: The Program Facilitator(s) can be a principal, a professor, a school teacher or therapist, or the Authorized Purchaser may also fill this role. The

Program Facilitator(s) determines what apps and what quantities to purchase, then calculates the cash value of the needed applications to submit to the Authorized Purchaser. The Program Facilitator is also the person who redeems the vouchers in the App Store Volume Purchase Program, and distributes the app-specific codes as necessary to the end users. In addition, the Program Facilitator(s) is responsible for keeping records of activation codes for each device onto which an app is installed. *Be Aware: Apple reserves the right to audit purchases to make sure that institutions are following usage rules, terms, and conditions.

4. End User(s): Apple divides end users into three different categories:

a. Single user (school account): Codes are distributed and redeemed by single users on a school-managed iTunes account.

b. Classroom or multiple users (assume a classroom of 30): Thirty codes are purchased for a classroom. One code is redeemed to a single iTunes account. That account can be authorized on up to five computers. The teacher can then synch all 30 devices using one code. The remaining 29 codes are kept on file in the event of an audit.

c. Single user (personal account): The school purchases vouchers and distributes codes to individuals. Each user redeems a code using their own personal iTunes account and installs the app onto their personal device. That app becomes the property of the student.

Volume Purchase Program
Step-by-Step Instructions _____

1. The Authorized Purchaser registers for a K12 School Account with the Apple Store. After the account is processed, Apple will forward an email to the Authorized Purchaser to confirm the account.

2. The Authorized purchaser will be responsible for purchasing vouchers from Apple for use with the volume purchase website.

3. The designated person will complete the Program Manager enrollment process and receive an email within 3-5 days containing a link to Apple's Program Facilitator web portal. The Program will designate unused Apple IDs for use by Program Facilitators. (Apple recommends the institution create non-personal email addresses for the Program Manager and Program Facilitator roles.)

4. The Program Facilitator can then log onto the volume purchase website and redeem vouchers purchased by the Apple Authorized purchaser. Depending on your workflow, it may be more efficient to search for the desired apps, determine the cost related to the required apps, and request a voucher from your Apple Authorized purchaser that would cover the total cost of the apps discovered.

5. The Authorized Purchaser then places an order for the type of Volume Voucher and Quantity based on the quote from the Program Facilitator. Volume Vouchers can be purchased in denominations of $100, $500, $1000, $5000 and $10,000 and may be purchased with a purchase order in addition to more conventional methods . The institution's tax status will be recognized and billed accordingly. Volume Vouchers

will arrive via snail mail in 3-5 business days. The Authorized Purchaser will then deliver the vouchers to the Program Facilitator(s).

6. The Program Facilitator(s) can then redeem the vouchers at the App Store Volume Purchase Program by entering a 16-digit code found on the back of the voucher (similar to an iTunes card). Once the purchase is complete the Program Facilitator(s) will receive an email with a link to a dashboard, now populated with app-specific codes. These codes can be distributed to users for redemption at the App Store.

*Notes:

- Keep track: create a spreadsheet of codes for audit purposes.
- The App Store Volume Purchase Program requires Program Managers and Program Facilitators to use a new, unique Apple ID specifically for this program. A non-personal email alias works best in this situation and can be easily created by your system administrator. These accounts will not be able to access the iTunes store to download applications, music, or any other content.

The Volume Purchase Program can be that simple. However, there are many individual intricacies and scenarios that will not be covered by the explanation above. Therefore, here is contact information for the Apple Volume Purchase Plan's experts (aka "the horse's mouth").

- Apple at 1-800-800-APPLE (1-800-800-2775 option 4, then option 3).
- www.apple.com/itunes/education
- http://developer.apple.com/support/ios/volume-purchase-program

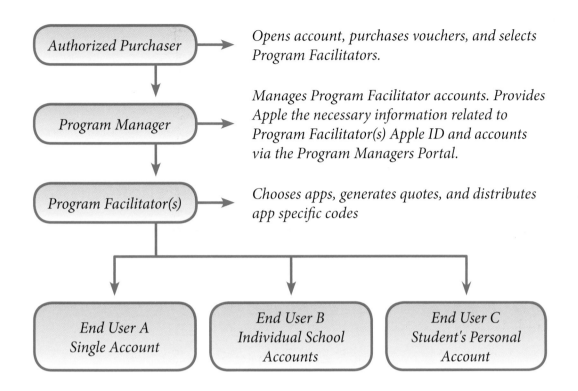

Part I

Apps to Get the Word(s) Out

Who would have thought that Apple would be the company to design the best, sleekest, most stylish, coolest communication devices to date? Not only do they entertain via books, movies, magazines, music, and videos, but the iPad, iPod touch, and iPhone have the muscle to be serious communication and educational devices. Whether you are using voice output, building vocabulary, correcting articulation, or strengthening muscle coordination, your iDevice makes it easier, more fun, and reinforcing. My students will sit quietly and wait in line for a chance to use these "magical" devices for just a few minutes.

This section presents applications that will turn your iDevice into a voice output, sign language, sentence generating, articulating paragon of communication. Individuals will be able to communicate and share thoughts and feelings in lieu of frustration and behavior challenges.

According to the Centers for Disease Control, it is estimated that 1 out of 110 children will be diagnosed with an autism spectrum disorder. Studies indicate that up to 60% of these children will be unable to communicate their wants, needs, and thoughts verbally. This means that up to 17,000 children are born each year who will be diagnosed with autism and remain functionally nonverbal.

So let's get down to the business of communication. Let's give individuals who have difficulty communicating the ability to say what they want to say, when they want to say it, through access to a multitude of words, signs, gestures, and vocalizations. A new way to communicate lies ahead!

Chapter 1: Voice Output

Voice Output applications are speech-generating apps that support individuals who are unable to use natural speech to meet all of their communication needs.

Success Story: Gaston

Gaston is my first student to use an iDevice for communication. He is a highly socially sensitive teenage boy, and although cognitively intact, he has significant challenges making his wants, needs, and requests known. For years Assistive Technology specialists have searched for ways to meet Gaston's unique communication needs. He was able to utilize a Pathfinder device effectively; however, he refused to use it after about a year because it made him look different. His dysarthric speech is highly unintelligible, yet he makes every attempt to communicate via verbalizations. Gaston is a socially aware teenager and is not comfortable showing others his weaknesses (reading and writing); therefore, he refuses to do either.

While searching the Internet for solutions to Gaston's unique communication requirements I came across a revolutionary idea: *Proloquo2Go*, developed by David Niemeijer and Samuel Sennott. When Gaston saw that he could communicate via iPhone, he was so ecstatic he cried. We immediately customized the *Proloquo2Go* to fit his needs, added pictures, and read through the manual together. That day on the bus ride home, Gaston texted his mother, "I will be home soon. I had a good day." Gaston's mother cried, and the next week, Gaston had his own iPhone. Success!

Success Story: Katrina

S ue M. has her own success story to tell about her daughter, Katrina: "A little more than a year ago, I was on a plane flying to Disney World with my family and doing something I would have thought was impossible. During the flight, I programmed a category for each Disney park and our resort on my daughter's iPod touch and *Proloquo2Go*. Five categories with at least 12 buttons each, without a manual, with pictures I had downloaded painlessly by wi-fi before we left home. And, I finished in time to use the iPod to play a few games before the flight landed. It was amazingly easy for someone who had used other devices that were painful to program (even with the manual).

And, on that trip, my daughter did something she had never done before in her whole life, even though she has had communication devices for quite a few years. She used her iPod device to talk to a stranger and order lunch. She had a cool device and she felt like using it to show people that she was cool too."

Katrina and her "cool" iPod touch

PROLOQUO2GO

by AssistiveWare

www.assistiveware.com

$189.99

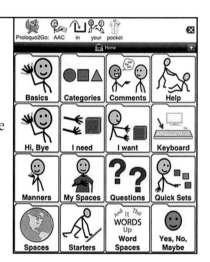

FROM THE DEVELOPER

Proloquo2Go™ is a new product from AssistiveWare that provides a full-featured communication solution for people who have difficulty speaking. It brings natural sounding text-to-speech voices, up-to-date symbols, powerful automatic conjugations, a default vocabulary of over 7000 items, full expandability and extreme ease of use to the iPhone, iPod touch and iPad.

CUSTOMER REVIEW

Thank you *Proloquo2Go*! Not only is this a fabulous app with high quality voice output system, moreover, *Proloquo2Go* has opened doors for new technology to be taken seriously. Finally, technology that fits individuals with autism at a reasonable price. *Proloquo2Go* is portable and lets individuals with disabilities be COOL. The *Proloquo2Go* website has two very helpful links. The first is the user forum. This is a place where individuals can relate useful information, tell personal stories and ask questions of other users (this is where I first got hooked). The second is for a brand new, easy-to-use set of tutorials, www.proloquo2go.com/Manual/article/downloadable-tutorials, covering everything from appearance to voice and pronunciation. AssistiveWare, please make a beginner version of *Proloquo2Go* for beginners that does not require such a powerful app.

 ## Success Story: Igor

My colleague and friend, Harumi Kato, a Speech Language Pathologist, has an amazing success story about using the iPod touch in conjunction with the *Proloquo2Go*: "Igor began therapy with Harumi when he was 13 years old. He had no verbal language and was able to identify three pictures (Goldfish, book, and bathroom). She started using the Tech Talk 32 with Igor and taught him colors, shapes, and requesting. It was soon obvious that the Tech Talk was limiting, bulky, and Igor was becoming averse to using it. Harumi began using her iPod touch with *Proloquo2Go* to support Igor's communication. Igor loved it! To make a long story short, Igor now has a 300+ word vocabulary and his average sentence is four to six words. And, the most amazing thing, at 13 years of age, Igor gained enough confidence to attempt verbal communication and can communicate with three-word utterances." Way to go, Harumi!

MY CHOICE BOARD

by Good Karma Applications, Inc

www.goodkarmaapplications.com/

$9.99

FROM THE DEVELOPER

The primary purpose of *My Choice Board* is to present a visual display of "choices" to those with limited communication skills. This gives individuals with autism, communication delays, or learning differences the opportunity to be independent and express their own specific needs and wants.

CUSTOMER REVIEW

My Choice Board is a great option for nonverbal students to communicate their desires. The user will find it easy to customize the pictures, boards, and audio to reflect an individual's wants and needs. Pictures can be uploaded from a computer, iPod touch or iPhone camera. Kudos to Good Karma for adding the "unavailable" option to visually emphasize what choices are not currently available.

 There is only one carrier phrase: "I Want." I want more carrier phrases!

MYTALK MOBILE

by 2nd Half Enterprises LLC

www.mytalktools.com/dnn

$39.99

FROM THE DEVELOPER

MyTalk Mobile for the iPhone, iPod touch, and iPad enables people with communication difficulties to express their needs and desires to those around them. Your purchase provides access to both *MyTalk Mobile* and *MyTalk Workspace*. Together, they represent a major breakthrough in augmentative, alternative communications (AAC) by making it easy to customize how you communicate through a variety of images, pictures, symbols, and audio files, including the human voice.

CUSTOMER REVIEW

I was surprised that the setup was not as complicated as it initially seemed. *MyTalk* was easy to customize. *MyTalk* has an optional companion web application/sync that allows the user to personalize voice, visual language sets, social stories, or story boards. The text-to-speech feature allows the user more flexibility during conversations and naturally occurring situations. Once you sign up for the website ($9.00 month, $75.00 year, or $175.00 for 3 years), you can create private pages using an image library or your own photos and store all content safely on the web. Support was friendly and helpful.

 Users will want to customize this app to fit their individual needs; it is not a load and go. Try the free version and view the Demo!

Kari Valentine, an occupational therapist with Wholistic Therapy Services in Nebraska has this to say about *MyTalk* and Heidi: "I am currently using *MyTalk* with a five-year-old, nonverbal female. She knows immediately when she sees the iPad that it can be used to communicate for her. She takes it and is able to hold it and press up to nine buttons to ask for what she wants. She has even figured out how to press the cancel button to navigate back to the last page. She is in Kindergarten.

There was some question about whether she could attach meaning to pictures, so teachers basically used sign language. She knows all her colors, a majority of her letters, and now using *MyTalk* she is able to tell people what she knows, so there is no denying that she is smart. She also is able to sign about 50 different signs. The only thing we have not figured out with our student is how to calm her when we have to take the iPad away; she throws a huge fit because she wants it with her all the time.

Heidi uses MyTalk to make a

presentation to her classmates.

LOOK2LEARN - AAC

by MDR

www.*look2learn*.com/*look2learn*/Home.html

$14.99

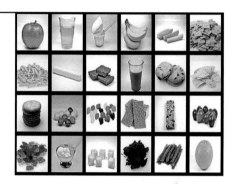

FROM THE DEVELOPER

Look2Learn (L2L), a revolutionary AAC software application for the iPod touch, iPhone, and iPad allows individuals to work at their communicative level using photographs to express wants and needs.

The easy-to-use system integrates preloaded vocal output so that individuals can use their "voice." In addition, users are able to record their own personalized audio and pair it with photos!

CUSTOMER REVIEW

Look2Learn has the potential to be awesome with clear, bold pictures and graphics. Eighty pictures come in three sizes and six categories. Tutorials are provided on the website and are easy to follow. Custom graphics and custom audio are available so that users can record their own voices and use personal photos. The *Look2Learn* app features a preloaded voice with good articulation and is easy to use. Good for beginning Assistive Technology users.

 Look2Learn could use more than one starter phrase ("I want").

iCONVERSE-ASSISTED COMMUNICATION

by Xcellent Creations, Inc.

www.converseapp.com

$9.99

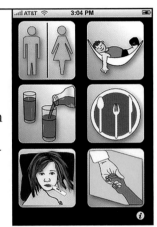

FROM THE DEVELOPER

iConverse–Assisted Communication is an educational tool designed for young children and individuals with communication disabilities, and toddler-aged children. *iConverse* is an Augmentative Alternative Communication (AAC) application that replaces bulky and expensive communication devices used in the past.

CUSTOMER REVIEW

This app is very nice. It gives six basic, clear, pictures. You have the option to program your own pictures with voice buttons (similar to a Go Talk 6). Suggested for expressing basic needs or, better yet, a parent/caregiver has the option of personalizing wants, needs and story boards. *iConverse* is recommended for beginning assisted communication users.

 Be on the lookout for future updates.

GRACE: PICTURE EXCHANGE FOR NON-VERBAL PEOPLE

by Steven Troughton-Smith

www.steventroughtonsmith.com/grace

$37.99

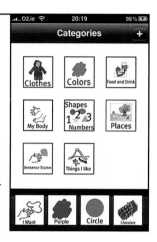

FROM THE DEVELOPER

A simple picture exchange system developed by and for nonverbal people, allowing users to communicate their needs by building sentences from relevant images. It can be customized by the individual using their picture and photo vocabulary, with the user taking and saving pictures independently to the app.

CUSTOMER REVIEW

Grace is a very simple picture exchange system for the iDevice. Custom pictures can be added easily.

 There is no audio. The developer suggests that it ensures interaction of the user with the listener.

LOCABULARY LITE

by puchApps LLC

www.locabulary.com

FREE

FROM THE DEVELOPER

Locabulary is an app developed for communication, information, and fun. Words are made available based on your GPS location. You can create a fast sentence using *Locabulary*'s noun-verb-object structuring. With *Locabulary*, you can easily speak the right words in the right place.

CUSTOMER REVIEW

I am looking forward to future versions. This app is great for building sentences. Few pictures included. It is perfect for communicating with words, phrases and sentences. Male or female voice options. My students prefer the female voice. The best feature is the Locabulate Me button. This button will provide the user with a map and restaurant choices in the area. *Locabulary* also has a nice text-to-speech keyboard. Last great feature is the font-size button. Fonts can be magnified easily from the home screen. Recommended for readers or beginning readers.

iPACS

by AdastraSoft

www.adastrasoft.com

$9.99

FROM THE DEVELOPER

It allows any user to customize information in various orders/ groups, or forms, to address different educational needs. In its simplest form, *iPACS* could mimic (with flexibility and functions going way beyond) traditional PECS book and specialized assistive communication devices that typically cost hundreds if not thousands of dollars.

CUSTOMER REVIEW

iPACS (Interactive Picture Assisted Communication System) can be conveniently organized like a picture exchange binder and used in a similar manner. A colleague of mine used the phrase, "PECS gone high tech." This app requires customization from the user.

 Students can easily or unintentionally change the settings.

VOICE4U

by Spectrum Visions

http://*voice4u*aac.com

$29.99

FROM THE DEVELOPER

Voice4u, is a revolutionary Augmentative and Alternative Communication (AAC) application that helps individuals to express their feelings, thoughts, actions, and things they need. It is a perfect solution for learning and communication for individuals with autism and the people around them.

CUSTOMER REVIEW

Voice4u is a load and go app. Using a combination of pictures and endearing drawings the user can express feelings as well as needs almost instantly. *Voice4u* only generates one-word phrases, kind of like flashcards. First choose an icon from the home page, then, on the second page, touch the icon for audio. Audio, image, and graphics can be easily customized. Recommended for beginning users.

 Current audio is breathy and the rate is a bit quick. User will want to customize audio.

EXPRESSIONIST

by AdastraSoft

www.adastrasoft.com

$9.99

FROM THE DEVELOPER

Expressionist is designed to help users to express, and to help users to model expressions. *Expressionist* stands out by using only the highest quality pictures and avoiding secondary references (such as using "snail" or "turtle" to represent "slow").

CUSTOMER REVIEW

I really like the idea of this app. The *Expressionist* app uses many starter phrases combined with pictures and an animation to communicate. Lots of choices. The designer claims that pictures avoid secondary references and indeed they do. An apple does not mean eat, an apple means just that, an apple. The animations use facial expression and gestures enhance understanding. Composite pictures replace sentence strips, so what you see is what you get.

 Because the format of *Expressionist* is different from most voice output apps, it is initially difficult to navigate. Also, *Expressionist* is glitchy. The screen jumps around, there are scrolling issues and voice output produces only part of the sentence.

Chapter 2: Sign Language

Sign Language is a visual-gestural system of communication. Sign Language was originally developed as a means of communication for the deaf and hard-of-hearing community. Likewise, it is a viable mode of communication for nonverbal individuals and those with emerging speech.

Success Story: Colin

Lightning struck twice for Colin. He is both deaf and autistic. When the only signer in his classroom left on maternity leave, Colin had no means of communication. He refused to use picture exchange and has limited reading and writing skills. We began utilizing Sign 4 Me, Smart Hands, and ABC Sign for Colin and the teaching staff. With the use of these three apps, Colin and his teachers are able to make wants/needs known and continue making progress on his goals. Bridge Built!

SIGN 4 ME - A SIGNED ENGLISH TRANSLATOR

by Vcom3D

http://signingapp.com

$9.99

FROM THE DEVELOPER

Vcom3D, the original developer of sign language software using SigningAvatar® characters, wants you to be able to learn sign language the way you need to communicate. If you have friends or a co-worker who is deaf or hard-of-hearing, now you can learn signs to communicate with them. The playback is in Signed English for the hearing person who wants to learn basic sign.

CUSTOMER REVIEW

According to the developers, *Sign 4 Me* was designed to be the ultimate tool for learning sign language. For my student who is deaf and has autism, *Sign 4 Me* is his only means of communication. There are many people in his environment who do not know sign language, therefore, *Sign 4 Me* bridges the gap from him to us and back. To use *Sign 4 Me*, simply type in a word, phrase or sentences and the avatar will sign it for you (text to sign. Your entries will be saved alphabetically into history for easy reference). An indispensable feature of this app is that the user can adjust signing speeds and rotate the avatar for the best view of hand shapes and movements.

 Sign 4 Me uses SEE (Signed Exact English) not ASL.

iSIGN

by iDev2.com

www.idev2.com

$4.99

few

FROM THE DEVELOPER

iSign is an animated phrase book of 800 American Sign Language (ASL) gestures. Each of the gestures is modeled with a 3D character and completely animated. The vantage point for each sign was chosen so that the user can see the details of the hand positions. These are the ASL signs, not finger spellings.

CUSTOMER REVIEW

iSign is an effortless app to use for acquiring American Sign Language vocabulary. I like the quiz section even though the sound effects startle me every time. The signing 3D characters are clear and precise, although a little stern. I found *iSign* to be clear, easy-to-use with good design and no glitches.

 There are no phrases or sentences. Check out the free version or the demo at http://iDev2.com/iSign-new.mp4. The only thing missing is the alphabet and numbers one through ten.

ABC SIGN

by iDev2.com

www.idev2.com/ABCsign/ABCsign.html

$0.99

FROM THE DEVELOPER

ABC Sign is an application designed to help children to learn the American Sign Language alphabet. Beautiful, colorful photographs illustrate each sign. A letter is spoken aloud and the user is presented with three choices for the correct sign. You can choose until the correct sign is found. A reward sound is played and the user can move to the next letter. Note: 25% of the profits from this application will be donated to help support deaf artists.

CUSTOMER REVIEW

ABC Sign is fantastic for learning the American Sign Language alphabet! Beautiful, clear screen shots. *ABC Sign* has both a learning mode and a quiz mode. The audio is breathy and the rate can drag a bit; however, it is intelligible and does get the job done. I wish it had the numbers one through twenty.

MY SMART HANDS BABY SIGN LANGUAGE DICTIONARY

by My Smart Hands

http://mysmarthands.com/Site/iPhone_MSH_Dictionary.html

$4.99

FROM THE DEVELOPER

Want a sign language tool that you and your baby can use together? *My Smart Hands Baby Sign Language Dictionary* teaches you and your little one the 300 ASL signs you need to know for clear communication.

CUSTOMER REVIEW

My Smart Hands Baby Sign Language Dictionary is the app my co-workers use when they want to learn a new sign. Not only do you see the sign clearly, there are verbal instructions for making the correct hand shapes. *My Smart Hands* is not just for babies. I use it for adult learners and students alike. A desired feature is the favorites list. This feature lets the user target specific signs for more concentrated practice. Test your knowledge by taking a quiz. *My Smart Hands* is easy to navigate, clear video, good audio with quiz and favorites features. I would recommend this app to anyone learning ASL vocabulary, even babies. Now you can convey, declare, inform, answer, and be heard with one touch of a finger. One-touch switches allow users to communicate whole messages with one easy touch. I have assembled an array of serious and fun switches to choose from. Choose the best one for your needs or choose them all.

Chapter 3:
One-Touch Switch

Now you can convey, declare, inform, answer, and be heard with one touch of a finger. One-touch switches allow users to communicate whole messages with one easy touch. I have assembled an array of serious and fun switches to choose from. Choose the best one for your needs or choose them all.

In the News

iPod touch Helps Kids with Autism Learn to Speak, Communicate

—by Alana Greenfogel

Parents and teachers of children with autism and other verbal disabilities know how challenging it can be at times to communicate with their kids. That's changing at schools in Plymouth with the help of the iPod touch.

Paulina is a kindergartener. She sits at a table with other students, coloring her assignment, but she needs the help of an aide because she can't speak. Well, she couldn't speak until a few weeks ago when she started using the iPod touch.

Paulina can answer her aides' and teachers' questions or indicate how she's feeling by pushing the buttons on the iPod. She can say "she's hungry" or "has to go to the bathroom" or she can say something as simple as she "wants to use the green crayon."

This is a tangible, hands-on learning tool that connects with the kids more than other types of therapy. The schools' aides and speech pathologist say they've never seen progress quite like this before. Hearing the iPod's voice has encouraged the kids to repeat the words on their own.

"Just in these couple of weeks she's had great progress with the words that she can use and the phrases she can say," says Michelle Richter, Paulina's aide.

"They are frustrated. They know what they want to say but they're just not able to express themselves," says Rita Large, the district's speech pathologist. "I love technology because it's so exciting and it lets us do so much more."

Large says grants and stimulus money paid for the iPods. She hopes one day every student who could benefit will have his or her own iPod, but that will require some financial help from parents.

TAPSPEAK BUTTON

by Ted Conley

http://conleysolutions.com/wordpress

$14.99

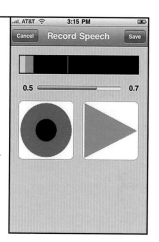

FROM THE DEVELOPER

TapSpeak Button modernizes the idea of a mechanical switch that records and plays messages. We have taken the idea and extended it to provide a portable, convenient, and stigma-free tool to use for basic teaching and communication tasks. *TapSpeak Button* is especially useful for teaching cause and effect relationships.

CUSTOMER REVIEW

If you use Switches or BigMac, you will love the *TapSpeak Button*. It is easy to program and will save favorite words or phrases for quick playback. The graphics are bright and clear. The developer has promised more products: *TapSpeak Sequences*, *TapSpeak Choices*, and *TapSpeak Pictures*. I am anxiously awaiting their debut.

TapSpeak Button can give only one message at a time. The user has to either record another or choose from a play list (user creates play list) to produce a different message.

TAPSPEAK SEQUENCE FOR IPAD

by Ted Conley

http://conleysolutions.com

$29.99

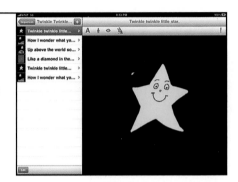

FROM THE DEVELOPER

Use *TapSpeak Sequence* instead of sequential message switches to record and customize messages without losing any previously recorded sequences.

CUSTOMER REVIEW

Sequence a social scenario, song, circle time, task analysis, and story books so that everyone can participate. *TapSpeak Sequence* for iPad gives unlimited sequencing abilities for optimal customization and picture support for the phrase/sentence. TapSpeak apps have switch support courtesy of RJ Cooper.

ANSWERS:YESNO

by SimplifiedTouch

www.simplifiedtouch.com/SimplifiedTouch

$0.99

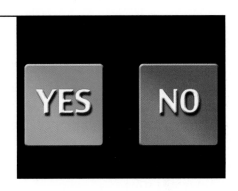

FROM THE DEVELOPER

Answers:YesNo was designed with one purpose in mind. Provide an easy to use, affordable way for a nonverbal young man with autism and motor planning issues to communicate with those around him.

The application is straightforward. It has two, large, color-coordinated buttons: one for yes, and one for no. Press either, and you will hear a voice read your selection.

CUSTOMER REVIEW

That's it, simply yes or no. If your student is nonverbal and understands or is working on the concepts of yes and no you must have this app. The three voice options are super articulate and clear. The cartoon voice is usually preferred by all.

SOUND MACHINE PRO

by MountainDev

http://mountaindev.blogspot.com

$2.99

FROM THE DEVELOPER

The biggest sound app of its kind! Unleash more than 50 high quality sound effects with the tap of your finger!

CUSTOMER REVIEW

Everybody enjoys using sound effects to make a statement. One sound effect can communicate 100 words. The sound of crickets, a yawn or snoring all convey a very clear message. Let's give everyone, verbal and nonverbal, the opportunity to be funny or a weisenheimer.

 Sound Machine Pro has some sound effects that may be offensive (burp or fart). Try the free version, then decide.

VOICE CHANGER PLUS

by Arf Software Inc.

www.arfsoftware.com

FREE

FROM THE DEVELOPER

Would you like to change your voice in strange and wonderful ways? *Voice Changer Plus* lets you do just that!

CUSTOMER REVIEW

Voice Changer Plus is a tool I use to motivate verbal expression. Students record their voices and then change the sound effects.

Voice Changer Plus can also be used as a switch to communicate a single thought or build a library of recordings to play at appropriate times. Given the opportunity, many students like adding humorous effects to their messages. Messages can be saved and used for social networking to family or friends.

 The user needs to speak slowly and clearly into the microphone for best results. The audio is fair to good.

SAY WHAT!?!

by Marmot Kilt Software

www.marmotkilt.com/Site

$1.99

FROM THE DEVELOPER

Your photo "speaks" the sound while the mouth moves in perfect rhythm. If you want to add a talking mouth to any photo, why haven't you already purchased *Say What!?!* You say you don't want to add a talking mouth to your photos? That just means you haven't seen a talking mouth in a photo before.

CUSTOMER REVIEW

Anyone or anything can give any message. *Say What!?!* is an easy-to-use app that lets the user create talking pictures. Use with sample photos or take your own snapshots. Simply choose size and shape of mouth, record and play back. Voila, a talking photo. I have taken pictures of nonverbal students and recorded words or phrases to share with others. The students like it so much that they will try to imitate it. It is a great motivator for verbal output and can be used like a switch to relay information.

Edit Mode 1, 2, and 3, which allow the user to set the size, shape, and rotation of the mouth box are tricky at first. Just remember, touch inside the shaded area to move the mouth and outside the shaded area to shape and rotate the mouth. Have fun and try the free version first. Recommended as a means to encourage verbal expression or as a unique personalized switch to communicate information. *Say What!?!* Messages can be shared on your YouTube account.

SKULL

by Arf Software Inc.

http://arfsoftware.com/Skull/Skull.html

FREE

FROM THE DEVELOPER

Skull includes a fully featured voice changer. You can record your own voice, sounds, and change the pitch up or down, add echoes, special effects, and more!

CUSTOMER REVIEW

The *Skull* app gives users the opportunity to personalize messages and stay topical during the fall season. Use *Skull* in the same manner as a switch. Messages, jokes, comments, or movie lines can be customized, saved, and played back with a shake or double tap.

 Preselected messages are played in order. Selecting a specific message for an occasion takes filing through the phrases page and resetting. It's free; why not add this app to the list of voice output apps and give users an opportunity to show their personalities?

Chapter 4: Text-to-Speech

With text-to-speech applications, you can convert written text into spoken words, spoken words into text, thoughts to text, or text into a talking bald guy!

iBALDI

by Animated Speech Corporation

www.animatedspeech.com/iPhonebaldi.html

$0.99

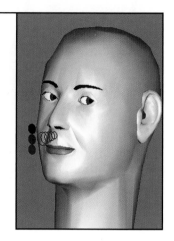

FROM THE DEVELOPER

Watch and listen to *iBaldi*, a 3D animated character who can read you text with extraordinarily accurate mouth and face movements and convincing emotions.

CUSTOMER REVIEW

iBaldi is much more than a great text-to-speech app, he is an articulation coach and language tutor. *iBaldi* provides the user with an optional inside (medial) view to the articulators as he is speaking. Pretty cool tool for a speech pathologist. I was thrilled; however, my younger students did not share my excitement. They thought it was gross. *iBaldi* is fairly interactive as you can change his emotions, rate, and head position in space. All in all, this is one of the best, coolest apps around. I wish I had access to *iBaldi* when I was in grad school. Maybe I would have gotten a better grade in my articulation/phonology classes. Recommended for everyone, even grad students.

 iBaldi's speech is a bit robotic.

PREDICTABLE

by tbox apps

http://tboxapps.com

$159.99

FROM THE DEVELOPER

Predictable may be the valuable communication aid for people with conditions such as cerebral palsy, motor neuron disease, and acquired brain injury. Users can type a message more efficiently by using a sophisticated word prediction engine and speak the message using a range of voices.

CUSTOMER REVIEW

It's hard to ignore how important apps have become where communication is concerned. *Predictable* is perhaps one of the most robust and important apps in this category. With incredible word prediction, voice output, switch access, and scanning capabilities, *Predictable* is much more than text-to-speech; it is a sophisticated assistive technology app that allows the user the flexibility and tools needed to communicate more naturally in a variety of environments. Among the many features users have at their fingertips are: three modes of access (scan and switch, direct touch, and touch anywhere), customizable phrase bank, UK/USA dictionary, nine adjustable voices, social network, and email capabilities. This app must be considered when making assistive technology decisions. See for yourself by viewing the introduction to *Predictable* on the tbox website. Still not sure? Read through the downloadable user guide also provided on their website.

ASSISTIVE CHAT

by assistive apps

www.assistiveapps.com

$24.99

FROM THE DEVELOPER

Assistive apps presents *Assistive Chat*, an affordable Augmentative Alternative Communication (AAC) Device, catered toward people with difficulty in speech. The biggest challenge for such users when using AAC devices is the number of key strokes or hits required to construct any sentence. To overcome this challenge, *Assistive Chat* is designed to be simple and efficient, allowing users to communicate at the fastest rate possible, with natural sounding voices.

CUSTOMER REVIEW

Assistive Chat is an excellent word prediction/text-to-speech app. Some features of *Assistive Chat* are word prediction, adaptive learning of new vocabulary, three voices to choose from, favorites list, and a quick list. Word prediction supports individuals who have challenges retaining ideas in memory long enough to write them down, difficulty spelling, and motor impairments that make it difficult to write or use a keyboard effectively. Assistive apps, please provide a trial version.

DRAGON DICTATION

by Nuance Communications

www.dragonmobileapps.com

FREE

FROM THE DEVELOPER

Dragon Dictation is an easy-to-use voice recognition application powered by Dragon® NaturallySpeaking® that allows you to easily speak and instantly see your text or email messages. In fact, it's up to five times faster than typing on the keyboard.

CUSTOMER REVIEW

Dragon Dictation is not just for business productivity. It is a seriously good assistive technology speech-to-text transcription application. Speech-to-text allows users to give commands and enter data using their voices rather than a mouse or keyboard. Individuals with motor or vision challenges can take notes, write reports, send email, tweet, and access Facebook. Check the *Dragon Dictation* website for languages supported.

 The user must have clear speech to make use of *Dragon Dictation*.

TIKI'NOTES 6 KEYS FRIENDLY KEYBOARD NOTEPAD

by Tikilabs

http://tikilabs.com/app/tikinotes

FREE

FROM THE DEVELOPER

Tiki'Notes is using our exclusive Tiki6Keys™ mobile keyboard technology which has been developed specially to provide the user with an efficient typing interface.

CUSTOMER REVIEW

This six key typing experience was meant to enhance the typing experience for those who prefer to type with one hand. Moreover, *Tiki'Notes* has made it possible for individuals with motor control challenges to access the touch-screen keyboards on their iDevices. It is much easier to use six large buttons than a standard keyboard. An intuitive user-interface and display lets the user choose keyboard layouts, language, import/export of text and, best of all, word prediction. Once a message is created it can be emailed or posted to social networks. The whole app is incredibly robust and works just as you'd want it to. *Tiki'Notes* even features a "type and walk mode." If anyone finds a use for this feature please let me know what it is. *Tiki'Notes* supports more than 20 languages.

 The only drawback is the lack of text-to-speech. For all that, it's free!

SPEAK IT! TEXT-TO-SPEECH

by Future Apps Inc.

www.future-apps.net/main/Future_Apps.html

$1.99

FROM THE DEVELOPER

Future Apps presents *Speak it!*, the highest quality text-to-speech App available for the iPhone, iPod touch, and now iPad. *Speak it!* utilizes the same voice synthesis engine that has made our iSpeak translator apps such a great hit. The text-to-speech engine is so powerful, it reproduces speech that is clear and natural sounding. Copy emails, documents, web pages, PDF files, and more; paste them into *Speak it!*, You can even create the same quality audio files of the text-to-speech, which can then be emailed to anyone you like!

CUSTOMER REVIEW

What a bargain. This is one of the best text-to-speech apps I have heard. Two male and two female voices are featured with *Speak it!* I really enjoy the Brit voices. Easy to use and easy to store phrases for quick use. Be sure to set up your email account to send audio messages. I would recommend this TTS app to anyone who desires a good text-to-speech tool. *Be Aware: To access the settings and files, the iPad has to be in landscape mode. Additional voices and languages are available for an additional 99 cents.

iMEAN

by Michael Bergmann

www.imean.mobi/iMean_site

$4.99

FROM THE DEVELOPER

iMean turns iPad into a letter board with large, easy-to-read keys and word suggestions. I developed it to help my autistic son formulate and communicate his thoughts.

CUSTOMER REVIEW

iMean is a keyboard with word prediction. The word prediction feature gives three possible choices. *Be Aware: The three choices given in word prediction are not always the most popular choices. For example, when typing the word, "to," the three choices given with *iMean* are toad, toadded and toadding. I really wanted to type the word, "today." *iMean* has three keyboard choices: numeric, letters (QWERTY and ABC) and keyboard. Frequently used messages can be saved for convenience.

There is no voice output at this time. Stay tuned: The developer reports that he is exploring ways to streamline the audio so that the iPad can speak.

iSAYIT

by codeBuilder

www.codebuilder.co.uk

$0.99

FROM THE DEVELOPER

iSayIt lets you alter the pitch and speed of the output voice, allowing you to fine-tune the voice you hear. Favorite sayings can also be saved, giving you quick access to the things you want your phone to say.

CUSTOMER REVIEW

iSayIt is a text-to-speech application. It is more of a novelty than a serious TTS app. Can be fun as it allows the user to alter the voice a bit.

Success Story: Bret

Bret is perhaps the most poignant success story of all and the proof of why we must all continually strive to do better.

Bret was a new student in one of my junior high classrooms. He was considered nonverbal because his speech was very low and unintelligible. Bret would usually sit with his arms crossed with a look of frustration on his face. His communication goals were simply to use two- to four-word utterances to convey information via picture exchange and/or verbalizations. During a language group where the students were describing wax paper, Bret appeared to be attempting to make a comment. Each student had a chance to give one or two descriptors about wax paper. I heard all the right descriptors such as thin, smooth, clear, crinkly, etc. Bret again attempted to make a comment. The classroom teacher prompted Bret, "Speak up, so that we can hear you." This prompt did not help. Bret then crossed his arms and sat back in his chair with no further attempts to make a comment. Hmmmm, I think he may have heard this prompt a time or two. Luckily, I had my iPhone within reach. I opened a text-to-speech app and handed it to Bret. He immediately began to type the response, "Moisture resistant due to a thin layer of wax." OMG! The classroom fell silent and Bret smiled with pride. I think we should rethink and rewrite some goals for this young man. My students surprise me every day.

Chapter 5: Articulation

Articulation is the production of speech sounds. The American Speech-Language-Hearing Association defines Articulation Disorders as follows:

Most children make some mistakes as they learn to say new words. A speech sound disorder occurs when mistakes continue past a certain age. Every sound has a different range of ages when the child should make the sound correctly. An articulation disorder involves problems making sounds. Sounds can be substituted, left off, added, or changed. These errors may make it hard for people to understand you. Adults can also have speech sound disorders. Some adults continue to have problems from childhood, while others may develop speech problems after a stroke or head injury.

Articulation treatment may involve demonstrating how to produce the sound correctly, learning to recognize which sounds are correct and incorrect, and practicing sounds in different words.

SUNNY ARTICULATION TEST

by Smarty Ears

www.smarty-ears.com

$49.99

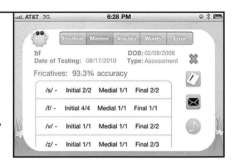

FROM THE DEVELOPER

The *Sunny Articulation Test* (SAT) is an individually administered clinical tool for screening, identification, diagnosis, and follow-up evaluation of articulation skills in English-speaking individuals. Administration time for the screening is between four and eight minutes. Administration of the full assessment is from 9–20 minutes.

CUSTOMER REVIEW

Bravo Smarty-Ears! *Sunny Articulation Test* makes the life of a Speech Pathologist a little bit easier and saves trees. *Sunny Articulation Test* is easy, portable, clear-cut and analyzes the data. This app can be used as a screening tool or full test. Smarty Ears provides anyone interested in this app with access to a video tutorial and downloadable manual. This is the future of testing, screening, data analysis, protocols, and is going to save me a lot of time. Recommended for busy speech-language pathologists.

VAST™-AUTISM 1-CORE

by SpeakinMotion™

www.proactivespeechtherapy.com (for further information on Autism 1-Core)

www.speakinmotion.com (for further information on *SpeakinMotion*)

$4.99

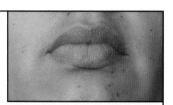

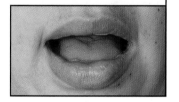

FROM THE DEVELOPER

I designed this app to work for individuals who have motor speech challenges and/or autism after seeing how extremely effective the VAST technique is with adult acquired apraxia and non-fluent aphasia. My colleagues and I have had amazing results with students on the spectrum as well as students with motor speech programming disorders.

CUSTOMER REVIEW

VAST™-Autism 1-Core provides unprecedented support for spoken language, combining evidence-based best practices and technology to deliver remarkable results.

VAST™-Autism 1-Core is a groundbreaking tool that provides state-of-the-art therapy to students with autism and motor speech programming disorders such as apraxia. *VAST™-Autism 1-Core* combines the highly effective concept of video modeling with written words and auditory cues to help individuals acquire relevant words, phrases, and sentences so that they can speak for themselves. For children and individuals with strong visual skills, this can be a key to developing speech.

VAST™ AUTISM 1-CORE (continued)

Videos are organized into a hierarchy of five categories beginning with syllables and ending with sentences. Each video gives a spoken target utterance that is preceded by the written word(s). Each word, phrase, and sentence is concrete and has meaning that can be generalized and practiced throughout the day. Providing the written word will prevent a student from labeling a picture of a frog jumping as "go," a person lying on a mat as "break time" or labeling a swing as "weee." The ability to recognize the written target word(s) will increase functional communication and enhance acquisition of spoken language. The progression of *VAST™-Autism 1-Core* Videos is as follows:

1. Syllable Repetition

2. Single Syllable Words

3. Multi-Syllabic Words

4. Phrases

5. Sentences

SMALLTALK PHONEMES &
SMALLTALK CONSONANT BLENDS

by Lingraphica

www.aphasia.com

FREE

FROM THE DEVELOPER

SmallTalk Phonemes and *SmallTalk Consonant Blends* provide a series of speech-exercise videos, each illustrating the tongue and lip movements necessary to produce a single phoneme and single consonant blend. With this app, people with apraxia, aphasia, and/or dysarthria resulting from stroke or head injury can easily practice the specific phonemes they need and repeat them as often as they like.

CUSTOMER REVIEW

SmallTalk phonemes and *SmallTalk Consonant Blends* are tools that every speech thera-pist should have access to. Video Modeling provides an effective method of teaching new skills, particularly if an individual avoids face-to-face interactions and can readily pro-cesses visual information. SmallTalk articulation series is highly recommended for indi-viduals of all ages who have difficulty producing single phonemes or consonant blends.

ARTIKPIX – FULL
by RinnApps

www.rinnapps.com/*artikpix*

$29.99

FROM THE DEVELOPER

ArtikPix has flashcard and matching activities to address articulation difficulties. The activities include features such as recorded audio, voice recording, and data collection to help children with speech sound delays. Children use *ArtikPix* to practice sounds independently, with a speech-language pathologist, or their parents.

CUSTOMER REVIEW

I do not hear groans anymore when I work on articulation. *ArtikPix* is a highly motivational articulation activity. Students learn correct articulation, labeling, and self-monitoring skills. Therapists and teachers get the luxury of having data taken automatically. *ArtikPix* features 21 customizable decks with

40 cards each, sound and visual settings, two modes of learning (flashcard and matching), audio recording, and data collection options. My students will complete a traditional articulation lesson to have access to *ArtikPix*. Essentially, they are working to work. Recommended for home, school, and independent practice.

POCKET SLP ARTICULATION

by Synapse Apps, LLC

http://pocketslp.com

$29.99

FROM THE DEVELOPER

Pocket SLP Articulation creates an engaging atmosphere by offering a unique multi-sensory approach to articulation drills. Presented with over 2,100 high-quality, carefully researched flashcards targeting both the word and sentence levels, clients and children are met with immediate auditory feedback, and are tacitly involved as they push buttons and/or swipe their way through the images. Pocket SLP offers 29 phoneme selections, seven of which are devoted to /r/ and its vocalic variations.

CUSTOMER REVIEW

Pocket SLP Articulation is a super tool for any therapist who works with articulation delays. No need to carry stacks of articulation flash cards, card decks, data sheets, pens, and pencils when all you need to remediate articulation errors is this app. Target phonemes can be in initial, medial, final position, or in short sentences. Users can score themselves with the help of the therapist or parent. Scores of correct, incorrect, and approximations are revealed in real time and a summary is provided and stored for each user upon completion. Pocket SLP features both a side and palate views of the articulators to help with placement. Articulation therapy just got easier and a whole lot more fun.

iSPEECHIMPROVER

by Futuristic Vision

http://sites.google.com/site/ispeechimprover

$1.99

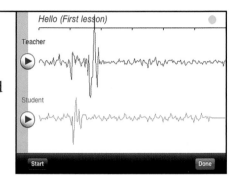

FROM THE DEVELOPER

iSpeechImprover is an easy-to-use and straightforward application that can help you significantly improve your speech and/or reduce your accent. The principle is based on the specifically developed algorithm that compares a user speech pattern with previously recorded speech pattern of the same word/phrase. The algorithm recognizes differences in two patterns and can evaluate user performance. Graphic representations of individual speech patterns are plotted on screen and can be assessed by users independently.

CUSTOMER REVIEW

This is a truly unique app. *iSpeechImprover* was originally meant for accent reduction; nonetheless, it has proven to be a valuable, affordable, visual support to refine articulation (hard of hearing and hearing), support individuals working towards a "socially acceptable" voice, and to rectify voice and motor speech disorders. The "Teacher" can create vocal templates for the student to practice with at their leisure. *iSpeechImprover* will even give the user a percent of correct responses, based on their production, in comparison to the target speech (30% = red circle, 65%=yellow circle, and 90%=green circle).

SLP MOBILE ARTICULATION PROBES

by Smarty Ears

www.smarty-ears.com

$24.99

FROM THE DEVELOPER

With *SLP Mobile Articulation Probes* you have access to over 936 words with their respective images at the touch of a button. This is a tool that can be used to complement your assessment information, to make progress in therapy, or to recommend to parents to complement therapy at home.

CUSTOMER REVIEW

Speech Pathologists, we no longer have to pack multiple decks of cards, data sheets and writing utensils everywhere we go. If your caseload has students with phonological process or articulation disorders, you need this app. An entire caseload can be entered and data tracked with *SLP Mobile Articulation Probes*. Just the fact that MAP takes and analyzes your data with just a touch,

makes this app worth its weight in gold. I spend a significant amount of "down time" collecting and analyzing data on a daily basis. I am hopeful that more apps will include this highly desirable feature. If you are unsure if MAP will meet your needs, check out the tutorial featured on the Smarty Ears website.

/R/ INTENSIVE SLP

by Smarty Ears

www.smarty-ears.com

$27.99

The Squirrel Is Eating Nuts

FROM THE DEVELOPER

With over 450 target words, */r/ intensive SLP* is the best tool for practicing this "interesting" phoneme. */r/ intensive SLP* uses a phonetic approach to teaching the "r" sound by creating subgroups that will hopefully make your student more successful in therapy. /r/intensive SLP is the only tool in the market that allows you not only to practice the production of the /r/ phoneme, but also to tally the percentage of accuracy at the same time with the same tool: your iPhone, iPad, or iPod touch.

CUSTOMER REVIEW

/r/ is a particularly difficult phoneme to remediate. */r/ intensive SLP* gives the Speech Pathologist all the tools necessary to remediate this complicated sound. If you have students who have trouble producing /r/, you need this app. */r/ intensive SLP* is a little expensive; however, the time it saves taking data and shuffling through flash cards is well worth the bucks.

iSPEECH

by Orange Driver Software

www.orangedriverapps.com

$3.99

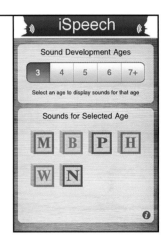

FROM THE DEVELOPER

Wrapped up in a fun and attractive user interface, sounds are organized by the ages at which they should have developed, giving you benchmarks for where your child should be developmentally. Any problem sounds can then be selected to display the teaching information for that sound.

CUSTOMER REVIEW

iSpeech for Articulation—Do not get this app mixed up with all the others that begin with *iSpeech*. This app is filled with information regarding the development of speech sounds. Recommended for parents, educators, and caregivers.

 This app is for informational purposes only. iSpeech offers tips and techniques to understand the developmental process of articulation and teach proper sound formation. There are no activities or corresponding pictures. Read the description and reviews prior to purchasing.

Chapter 6:
Encouragement

By the age of three, most children are able to use language to communicate their wants, needs, and make comments. Children with autism have difficulties with spoken language and struggle with communication throughout their lives. Given the encouragement to attempt verbalizations using innovative and highly motivating methods can make a significant positive impact on the eventual display of talent. And, since children are often more willing to communicate about things that interest them, utilizing high interest, encouraging apps will ensure a tremendous level of motivation and accomplishment. A little encouragement goes a long way.

PHOTOSPEAK

by MotionPortrait, Inc.

http://labs.mppark.jp/apps/photospeak.html

$0.99

FROM THE DEVELOPER

PhotoSpeak™ takes still photos and transforms them into amazing 3D avatars that can repeat your every word.

CUSTOMER REVIEW

How do they do that? *PhotoSpeak* literally brings your photos to life. The user can choose two modes of verbal playback: instant playback (voice is high-pitched and mouse-like) or pre-record your message (your voice). Just upload a full-face photo, talk to the photo and bring it to life. Your talking 3D avatar can deliver your message easily via email or social media with the tap of your finger. Included features let the user add glasses and curly hair with a double tap to the screen. The photo/avatars will even follow your finger around the screen with their eyes and head. The motivational and communicative uses are endless. Nonverbal students benefit from watching their photos talk and can then use *PhotoSpeak* as a switch. Pre-recorded messages can be saved for easy use. To get a better idea of the amazing nature of this app, watch the video tutorial on the developer's website.

iREVERSE SPEECH

by Apptomic LLC

www.apptomic.com/products

FREE

FROM THE DEVELOPER

This app allows you to record audio and then play the recording backwards.

CUSTOMER REVIEW

iReverse Speech does just that. Record any message and play it back, forward, or backward. *iReverse Speech* encourages verbal- izations, turn-taking, and is a marvelous reinforcer. Every student is fascinated by hearing their words in reverse and wants to make three or four recordings. Some students will make and record palindromes.

 This app runs an add banner. I can usually overlook an ad banner when the app is free. There is more than one use for this app, so be creative and enjoy!

TALKING CARL & TALKING TALKERS

by Awyse

(Carl) www.awyse.com/talkingcarl
(Talkers) www.awyse.com/talking-talkers

$0.99 (Carl) or FREE (Talkers)

FROM THE DEVELOPER

Talking Carl repeats anything you say with a hilarious voice. He can also be poked and pinched and you can even tickle him to make him laugh out loud. With Talking Talkers, you can customize and deliver crazy messages on video to your friends and family. Just a click and a tap away, *Talking Talkers* is always here to make you laugh when you feel sad or lonely.

CUSTOMER REVIEW

Both *Talking Carl* and *Talking Talkers* encourage expressive language. Simply say a word or phrase and they will repeat it. Both are bright, colorful, and cute. The user can tickle, poke, and pinch the characters to make them respond.

 Talking Carl and *Talking Talkers* have silly cartoon voices. The user cannot customize the voice. They were originally meant as novelty apps; however, they have become one of the best ways to inspire verbalizations and giggles from most students. With *Talking Talkers*, the user can record and send messages via email or social networking.

CRAZY FACE

by Ezone.com

http://iPhone.ezone.com

$0.99

FROM THE DEVELOPER

It's a whole motley crew of interactive monsters whenever you need them! You talk, *Crazy Face* moves—just swipe to choose from four different characters! Collect all the *Crazy Face* volumes today!

CUSTOMER REVIEW

Students will do anything to make the faces talk. With *Crazy Face*, the user can make four different, loveable monster faces talk (move their mouths up and down).

Crazy Face has no audio. The monsters merely move their mouths up and down as the user does the talking. This super-simple app can be utilized to motivate verbal expression or gain the attention of your listeners. If you like this app, try *Crazy Face–3 Little Pigs* or *Crazy Face–Snow White*. All *Crazy Face* apps come with a free version.

Part II

Receptive Language

"We were given two ears but only one mouth, because listening is twice as hard as talking,"

—Epictetus

Receptive language is listening and understanding what is communicated. Individuals with receptive language and/or auditory processing disorders may appear to be deaf or hard of hearing. They may mix up sounds or hear them incorrectly. This is usually related to the brain rather than the ear itself. The apps in this section can be used to strengthen auditory discrimination, processing, and receptive language skills. If we can encourage our students and children to listen more competently, they will be better communicators and have a greater quality of life. So let's be all ears and put on our thinking caps for better receptive language.

Chapter 7: Listening & Auditory Processing

Listening to something or someone and hearing them are two very different concepts. Just because we have heard a sound, word, or sentence doesn't mean it has registered in our brains. This is why teaching listening and auditory processing skills is so acutely important.

VOCAL ZOO GOLD +

by Funny i Games

http://vocalzoo.blogspot.com

$0.99

FROM THE DEVELOPER

Welcome to *Vocal Zoo Gold +*, the ultimate zoo experience for your kids. Here they can experience and learn about the world's most famous animals in the comfort of your home.

CUSTOMER REVIEW

Vocal Zoo Gold + is visually striking with 69 realistic animal sounds and pictures. Individuals can explore the app independently to improve auditory discrimination, vocabulary, and listening skills, or use it as a guessing game: "What animal makes this sound?" When students get good at listening, two or three animal sounds can be played consecutively or simultaneously to increase the difficulty. Two modes are available: The first is landscape. When the user holds the iPad in landscape mode there are six animals to a page. Touch an animal and hear the sound. Scroll up or down for more animals. In portrait mode, there is a single animal on the page. Touch the animal to hear its sound. Touch the word to hear its name. Scroll left or right for more animals.

I HEAR EWE - ANIMAL SOUNDS FOR TODDLERS

by Claireware Software

www.claireware.com

FREE

FROM THE DEVELOPER

Entertain and educate your toddler with this simple game full of 24 different authentic animal sounds and 12 different vehicle sounds. When your baby taps on an animal or vehicle icon, the game will verbally announce what type of animal or vehicle it is and play a recording of its real sound.

CUSTOMER REVIEW

Anyone working on auditory processing or listening skills will want this app. *I Hear Ewe* has 24 animal sounds and 12 vehicle sounds to sharpen auditory processing skills. Also, it's a good reinforcer—it's fun! I recommend turning off verbal descriptions ("This is the sound a _____ makes."). *I Hear Ewe* may even help you learn a second language as it comes in four languages. Did I mention? It's free!

MATCH

by Explorer-Technologies

www.explorer-technologies.com

$0.99

FROM THE DEVELOPER

This version of the classic matching game allows you to match icons/images and audio sounds as well. There are animal sounds, musical chords, and instruments.

CUSTOMER REVIEW

Anyone working on auditory discrimination, processing, and listening skills will want to have *Match* available. There are three auditory and one visual matching game. The audio is really very good. There are 16 squares per game with minimal bells and whistles. The user will want to start in a quiet environment and when he or she is really good at listening, move on to progressively noisier settings.

 No customization available. Four games with 16 squares each. The number of moves to finish the game and time elapsed are displayed on the bottom of the screen.

SOUND TOUCH

by SoundTouch

www.soundtouchinteractive.com

$2.99

FROM THE DEVELOPER

The app opens right to the activity, without a main menu. It's broken into six categories, which are shown at the bottom of the screen as pictures—animals, wild animals, wild birds, vehicles, musical instruments, and household. Each page has 12 items displayed with bright, cute, cartoon items. Tap a picture and a real life photo of the item pops open, accompanied by the sound it makes. Tap the picture anywhere, and it disappears.

CUSTOMER REVIEW

The photos in *Sound Touch* are fantastic, as is the sound quality. It is super simple to navigate and relies only on taps. *Sound Touch* is great for auditory processing or sound imitation activities. To support generalization, each sound has four different photos and four different sound bites. Highly recommended for auditory processing, auditory discrimination, labeling, describing, imitating, and just plain amusement.

SOUND MACHINE & ANIMALS SOUND MACHINE

by iFRizzo.com

http://ifrizzo.com

$0.99 each

FROM THE DEVELOPER

For those of you who want a personal sound effects library in the palm of your hand, *Sound Machine* is for you. Tell a joke and play a rim shot sound from your iPhone or iPod touch. If no one laughs (hey, that can happen) bring your own laughter!

CUSTOMER REVIEW

Sound Machine and *Animals Sound Machine* offer auditory processing, auditory discrimination, auditory games, and entertainment. Use *Sound Machine* apps just for fun and improve your auditory processing/listening skills at the same time! Individuals have fun making silly sounds with these apps and reproducing them vocally. Also, *Sound Machine* apps can be used as auditory guessing games. I have had students sit and file through the sounds reproducing each one quietly to themselves.

 What you see is what you get. *Sound Machine* is a simple app that cannot be customized or modified.

Chapter 8: Language Comprehension

"The limits of my language mean the limits of my world."

—Ludwig Wittgenstein

Language Comprehension is the ability to understand communication from others. Understanding spoken language requires complex auditory processing to translate speech into meaning. In this chapter you will find apps to support comprehension of the spoken word, following directions, critical thinking, and concept imagery. Practicing these skills will help our students understand and express their thoughts in an organized manner.

ABA RECEPTIVE IDENTIFICATION

by Kindergarten.com

http://kindergarten.com

$0.99 each

FROM THE DEVELOPER

Receptive language is the ability to understand and comprehend what is being said or read and is an essential part of language development. Understanding questions is the foundation for children to participate in conversations with others. Many children with emerging language skills do not think of things as having parts, attributes, or fitting into categories, but these are necessary for developing appropriate, functional conversation skills. Once a child can ask for, label, and receptively identify a great many items, it's a good time to start teaching the FFC's (Features, Function, and Class) of items, people, and places.

CUSTOMER REVIEW

There are five *ABA Receptive Identification* apps. Each app focuses on a different receptive language skill (identification, feature, function, class, and a combination). Pictures are clear and colorful with good audio. Reinforcement and encouragement are provided to keep the user motivated. The user is provided with three pictures and a verbal request: "Show me the one that is _____ ," or, "Find the one that _____ ." If the correct answer is chosen, verbal praise is provided. If you are incorrect, the question is repeated and the correct answer is revealed.

 There are no settings that allow vocabulary or concept choices. If this app had data tracking it would be awesome.

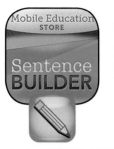

SENTENCE BUILDER & QUESTION BUILDER

by Mobile Education Tools

http://mobile-educationstore.com

$3.99 each

FROM THE DEVELOPER

Sentence Builder is designed to help elementary-aged children learn how to build grammatically correct sentences. Explicit attention is paid to the connector words that make up over 80% of the English language. *Question Builder* is designed to help elementary-aged children learn to answer abstract questions and create responses based on inference. Extensive use of audio clips promotes improved auditory processing for special needs children with autism spectrum disorders or sensory processing disorders.

CUSTOMER REVIEW

Sentence Builder and *Question Builder* are fun, engaging, and easy to use. Students can practice grammar and learn to answer questions independently. Levels can be set to match abilities. Animations are likeable and the multitude of reinforcements keeps students engaged. Each app tracks data! Both apps are recommended for students who can read fairly well. It would be wonderful if *Sentence Builder* and *Question Builder* came in a beginning level (hint, hint).

SENTENCE BUILDER & QUESTION BUILDER (continued)

Diana Zimmerman, MS, CCC-SLP, has this to say about *Sentence Builder*: "I love so much about this app! The dial format is engaging. I love the quick animations for correct answers. The animations are cute, funny, and quick! There is a man's voice that reads the sentence aloud after the correct answer and tells you to try again if you get it wrong. He speaks slowly and clearly and sounds real (not like a computerized voice). The graphics are simple but interesting. This can be used to address a variety of syntax errors in speech therapy. This would also be a nice way for kids to practice their syntax (grammar) at home. As a speech therapist, I can also target vocabulary by expanding on these sentences and pictures. Basic concepts can be targeted (example sentence: "He is skiing ... around the, up the, in the, before the, down the ... hill"). This app could be especially helpful for ESL students and SLI students."

"DreamsofTomorrow" agrees with Diana Zimmerman: "If you have a higher functioning autistic child who is leaving off the small words of sentences or using the wrong words, like one of mine is, this is a great app for him or her to get accustomed to putting those small words in with the appropriate words. I liked it enough that I bought an iPad and the iPad version. As a foster parent with seven autistic children in the home, I love the work put into programs like this. Keep up the good work!"

GUESS THIS ANIMAL: TEACHES AND QUIZZES ANIMAL FACTS

by Sprite Labs

www.animagik.com/AnimagikNewSite

$1.99

FROM THE DEVELOPER

Guess This Animal is an interactive application. Ranger Nora talks to your child throughout the app. She will either teach animal facts or play an animal guessing game with them.

CUSTOMER REVIEW

Students may think that they are playing a fun animal guessing game, but they are actually focusing on auditory memory and processing, as well as labeling and describing. *Guess This Animal* presents 32 animals in two modes: the first mode teaches animal facts and the second mode is for students to show their knowledge.

Ranger Nora is articulate with clear voice quality; however, she could use a little help with synching her lips to the audio track.

WHQUESTIONS

by Smarty Ears

www.smarty-ears.com

$13.99

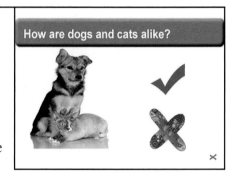
How are dogs and cats alike?

FROM THE DEVELOPER

Whquestions will provide you with over 300 "wh" questions in the following formats: "Where," "Who," "What," "How," and "Why." You will be able to choose the format you want to practice.

CUSTOMER REVIEW

WhQuestions is presented in a flashcard format. The user chooses the format, answers the questions and is provided with a percentage of correct answers.

This app is not meant to be used by the student independently. A therapist, teacher, or parent needs to be available to facilitate both the asking and answering of the "wh" questions. There is no audio with this app, so the user should have basic reading skills. *WhQuestions* is a handy (kind of expensive) tool for a traveling therapist who does not want to carry tons of flashcards from location to location. Check out the tutorial on the Smarty Ears website for additional information.

GUESS THE ANIMAL

by Cascade Management & Research LTD/Uri Elhav

www.m6dev.com/products/guess-the-animal

$0.99

FROM THE DEVELOPER

Guess the Animal teaches kids the names and voices of farm animals. Kids have fun learning to identify, name, and recognize over ten animals, including the horse, monkey, pig, cow, and more.

CUSTOMER REVIEW

One of the simplest language processing apps I will use. The user listens to and/or reads the prompt and chooses the correct animal from a choice of four. Simple!

Part III

Vocabulary and Concept Development

Learning vocabulary is important for any student, but it is doubly important for a student with autism. It is difficult to express your feelings, wants, and needs without specific words. An individual may be tired, ill, frightened, happy, or thirsty; however, without the vocabulary to express themselves, those feelings or desires may manifest themselves in behaviors.

Students with autism will learn more easily when material is presented in a simple, visual format. It is well known that if pictures are presented repeatedly, the student will learn and retain the info. Add the motivation of using a cool iDevice that an individual can freely explore and benefit from, and you have successfully expanded his or her perception of the world. Remember the words of Aristophanes, "By words the mind is winged."

Chapter 9: Vocabulary

A vocabulary is a set of words that an individual is familiar with and feels comfortable using while writing or speaking. Acquiring and expanding one's vocabulary is a life-long process and sometimes requires a singular effort. Ultimately, the investment in vocabulary-building pays off—providing a richer, deeper, and broader understanding of the world around us and allowing us to make fine distinctions among concepts, from the concrete to the figurative.

MARTHA SPEAKS DOG PARTY

by PBS KIDS

http://pbskids.org/mobile

$2.99

FROM THE DEVELOPER

A U.S. Department of Education-funded study found target vocabulary improved up to 31% for children ages three through seven who played this Parents' Choice Recommended app over a two-week period. Includes four fun-filled games starring Martha, the talking dog from the popular PBS KIDS TV series, Martha Speaks™.

CUSTOMER REVIEW

Martha Speaks Dog Party is evidence-based! Students learn vocabulary by engaging in three games and a pop quiz. Each game is led by Martha, the talking dog. Martha teaches vocabulary development through engaging games and activities. But that's not all; Martha is also supporting auditory processing, sequencing, creativity, and motor control. The audio and graphics are excellent. Enthusiastically recommended for individuals with vocabulary and auditory processing goals.

FIRSTWORDS: DELUXE

by Learning Touch

http://learningtouch.com/products

$4.99

FROM THE DEVELOPER

First Words: Deluxe is toddler-tested and approved, with a user interface designed specifically for the littlest of fingers. More than just a game, it is a sophisticated learning tool that engages children, encourages exploration, and helps them begin building a deep understanding of the relationships between letters and words.

CUSTOMER REVIEW

I do not know one student who does not find *First Words: Deluxe* irresistible. Students who show limited interest in the traditional "flash card" type of app will spend an entire session with First Words. Labeling, spelling, reading, eye-hand coordination, motor control, and smiles are all in one app! Users can customize the settings for speech, letter order, case, speed, and length. The audio is even good. My students and I have experienced such amazing results from First Words that I bought all versions.

AUTISM COLORS

by ZBobbApps.com

www.aba4autism.com

$19.99

FROM THE DEVELOPER

Dr. Gary Brown's *Autism Colors* app uses Discrete Trial Training (DTT) to help your child learn the basic colors. DTT is the primary teaching method used in Applied Behavior Analysis (ABA) to teach numerous pre-academic and social skills to children with autism. This app can be used to help teach the basic colors to children with autism, attention deficit disorder (ADD), attention deficit hyperactive disorder (ADHD), or any child who has trouble staying on task.

CUSTOMER REVIEW

Discrete Trial Training (DTT) is an evidence-based method used to teach children with autism. *Autism Colors* uses DTT to teach just that—colors. And, in the spirit of DTT, *Autism Colors* will keep track of your data. *Autism Colors* was designed for students on the spectrum; however, it can be utilized effectively for all students learning colors.

 ZBobbApps plans to offer several more apps in the near future.

AUTISM SHAPES

by ZBobbApps.com

www.aba4autism.com

$14.99

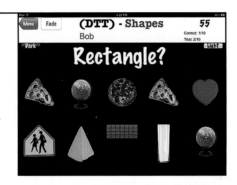

FROM THE DEVELOPER

This app uses Discrete Trial Training (DTT) to help your child learn the basic shapes. DTT is the primary teaching method used in Applied Behavior Analysis (ABA) to teach numerous pre-academic and social skills to children with autism. This app can be used to help teach the basic shapes to children with autism, attention deficit disorder (ADD), attention deficit hyperactive disorder (ADHD), or any child who has trouble staying on task.

CUSTOMER REVIEW

ZBobbApps has done a fantastic job in adapting Discrete Trial Training (DTT) to app format. If you have a student who learns via DTT and learning shapes is a goal, *Autism Shapes* is the right app for you. *Autism Shapes* is fully customizable with choices for shape, interval, number of choices provided, background, and language. It has been clinically tested and therapeutically designed to teach shapes and keep track of data. There are no distracting stimuli and reinforcement is minimal (verbal only).

ABA FLASH CARDS

by Kindergarten.com

http://kindergarten.com

FREE

Emotions

FROM THE DEVELOPER

At Kindergarten.com our flash cards are specifically created to stimulate learning and provide tools and strategies for creative, effective language building. *ABA Flash Cards* can be a great tool for fostering the mastery of new words, building vocabulary, and conveying new concepts.

A B C D E F G
H I J K L M N
O P Q R S T
U V W X Y Z

Alphabet

CUSTOMER REVIEW

ABA Flash Cards offers thirteen wonderful, high-quality sets of free flash cards. Sets range from shapes and ABCs to emotions and actions. Settings are limited to on/off for shuffle, voice, chime, and music reinforcement. Clear, articulate, and consistent audio is used throughout all 13 sets. Chimes and musical reinforcement are designed to keep students interested. These are awesome flash cards, but just that—flash cards.

Vegetables

Actions

 The "Fruits and Nuts" flash cards have foods that my students were not aware of (starfruit, rambutans, cactus pear). Cards cannot be deleted from or added to the decks.

WATCH ME LEARN FLASHCARDS

by Watch Me Learn

www.watchmelearn.com

$1.99

FROM THE DEVELOPER

Watch Me Learn Flashcards is a fun new way to learn expressive and receptive language. Complementing the renowned teaching videos by Watch Me Learn, *Flashcards* brings the objects and verbs from the videos to the iPhone and iPod touch.

CUSTOMER REVIEW

Watch Me Learn Flashcards is just that—flashcards. The user has the option to have the word spoken in English or Spanish. Watch Me Learn has done an excellent job with the audio. This app uses a clear, non-abrasive voice and beautiful, vibrant pictures. Flashcards are separated into five categories: objects, food, playtime, opposites, and verbs. *Watch Me Learn Flashcards* is a very well done set of high-tech flashcards.

WORD TOTZ-CREATE FLASHCARDS FOR YOUR TODDLER

by Ingenious Monkey

www.ingeniousmonkey.com/WordTotz.html

$1.99

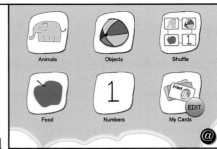

FROM THE DEVELOPER

WordTotz is a fun and customizable educational app for toddlers and preschool-aged children that helps them learn their first words using familiar pictures and sounds. With over 100 built-in cards containing vivid, full-color pictures and audio cues, *WordTotz* helps young children identify and learn words for everyday items around them: milk, dog, hand, chair, numbers, etc.

CUSTOMER REVIEW

WordTotz is easy to use and easy to customize. I was able to create a card (picture, audio, and graphics) in 11 seconds. The cards I create go into the My Cards pile. Pictures are clean and clear. The audio is not so clean and clear.

The user cannot edit existing categories, pictures, or graphics. I like the pictures; however, I would like to customize the audio.

iPRACTICE VERBS

by Smarty Ears

www.smarty-ears.com

$10.99

FROM THE DEVELOPER

iPractice Verbs makes practice fun because it allows you to flip through the images by shaking the iPhone or iPod touch, and for the more serious crowd it also allows you to progress simply by sliding your finger along the screen.

CUSTOMER REVIEW

iPractice Verbs provides the user with both a flashcard and audio in both word and phrase level. It would be great if it were a three to five second snippet of video for the verb as verbs are difficult to teach from a static picture. Smarty Ears offers a video tutorial on their website for those interested.

ANIMAL FUN

by Brian Pfeil

http://github.com/pfeilbr/animalfun

FREE

FROM THE DEVELOPER

Animal Fun is a simple animal learning program for children. Children learn about animals by seeing and hearing the sounds an animal makes. It combines an easy-to-use interface and fun sound effects to entertain children while they learn.

CUSTOMER REVIEW

Thank goodness it was free. The pictures are beautiful and the audio ... needs work. *Animal Fun* sounds like a See 'n Say from the '70s. However, my animal-loving students do not mind the sounds and like to look at, name, and spell the animals. Good enough for me!

Chapter 10:
Concept Development

Once your child or student has a 50-100 word vocabulary, it is time to introduce organization, or concepts. Individuals should begin learning and noticing that words have patterns and relationships to one another. There may be more than one meaning to a word and sometimes words don't mean what they say (figurative language). I have attempted to organize this chapter from basic to complex concepts.

I SEE EWE - A PRESCHOOLER WORD GAME

by Claireware Software

www.claireware.com

$0.99

FROM THE DEVELOPER

I See Ewe is an educational game that helps your preschooler learn to recognize over 50 different shapes, objects, colors, and animals, and exposes them to their first Sight Words. *I See Ewe* accomplishes this through two simple, yet fun and engaging, games.

CUSTOMER REVIEW

I See Ewe features vocabulary, concept development, and auditory processing in one easy-to-use app. *I See Ewe* can match your student's level by changing the number of choices and categories provided. There are five categories in all. Voiceover comes in four languages. Claireware, keep the great apps coming! This app is great for those who are beginning to focus on word relationships.

MISTER ROGERS MAKE A JOURNAL FOR PRESCHOOLERS

by PBS KIDS

http://pbskids.org/mobile

$1.99

FROM THE DEVELOPER

The Mister Rogers Make a Journal for Preschoolers app encourages children to identify and talk about their feelings and everyday experiences at school, playtime, and with friends. The app features an animated version of favorite "Neighborhood of Make-Believe" character Daniel Striped Tiger; he invites children to make a journal to help them reflect on the things they do and to express how they feel.

CUSTOMER REVIEW

Encourage your students to explore and learn how to describe their emotions. *Mister Rogers Make a Journal for Preschoolers* presents five journal topics; each journal has four pages. Each page gives the user a sentence starter and five choices to help describe his or her personal feelings. The last page is "freestyle" and users have the opportunity to create their own picture and graphics for the cover page. Journals can then be saved in the app library to read again later. *Mister Rogers Make a Journal* is an especially useful tool when used with a parent, caregiver, or educator who can help students talk about and share feelings.

LEARN TO TALK

by iLearn2Talk

www.ilearn2talk.com

$1.99

FROM THE DEVELOPER

Over 160 highly interactive, colorful flash cards engage and motivate toddlers to learn by themselves. For each lesson, your little one simply needs to swipe with his or her fingers to the left for the next card to appear or swipe to the right to go back one. As he or she flips through the cards, your child listens to, repeats, and learns the words and phrases.

CUSTOMER REVIEW

The *Learn to Talk* app is like having interactive flashcards that students can manage themselves. I show students once how to use this app and they are off and running. The audio sounds like it was recorded in a tunnel, but for some reason, students naturally want to repeat the words and like to listen to it. I found it easier to use when the spelling is turned off. The spelling feature can be distracting when students are learning the word(s). There is a nice progression from nouns, verbs, and one-word, two-word, and three-word phrases. The pictures could represent wider demographics. Recommended for beginning talkers, younger individuals, or the young at heart.

iTOUCHiLEARN WORDS FOR PRESCHOOL KIDS

by Staytoooned

www.staytoooned.com

$1.99

chick

igloo

sun

chick

goat

FROM THE DEVELOPER

iTouchiLearn Words for Preschool Kids features entertaining animations and engaging word games that teach your toddler and preschooler a series of words, spellings, and associated actions while making them laugh. Players receive virtual rewards for correct answers.

CUSTOMER REVIEW

iTouchiLearn Words is the first app I have found that gives the user a short animated movie to teach nouns, verbs, spelling, and Sight Words. *iTouchiLearn Words* is also an excellent tool for targeting receptive language skills. I have to recommend this app because of the animated approach to teaching language concepts and vocabulary. I am so excited about this app that I am not going to say anything objectionable about the audio. *iTouchiLearn Words* is divided into three sections: two focus on labeling/spelling and the third is a series of wonderful animations to teach nouns and verbs. Customization is minimal, background music and spell word options are available.

ABA PROBLEM SOLVING GAME

by Kindergarten.com

http://kindergarten.com

$0.99

FROM THE DEVELOPER

What skill could possibly be more useful than problem solving? Of all the valuable skills your child learns at school, problem solving should be number one. At Kindergarten.com we have developed a number of fun problem-solving applications to help young children develop these skills before they even start Kindergarten. These applications encourage creative problem solving, discrimination, and reasoning skills.

CUSTOMER REVIEW

ABA Problem Solving Games is a motivating alternative to flash cards. Pictures are bright and clear, with good audio. Your student or child is given a verbal prompt such as, "What does not belong?" and a choice of four answers. The right answer is rewarded with verbal praise, chimes, and a repetition of the correct answer. The wrong answer prompts the user to "try again." My students will use this app if I am sitting with them. When I leave, they change apps.

 The user is not provided the option of picking and choosing vocabulary and individualizing the lessons. It would be fantastic if this app collected data.

LANGUAGE BUILDER FOR iPAD

by Mobile Education Tools

http://mobile-educationstore.com

$3.99

FROM THE DEVELOPER

Language Builder offers a rich and fun environment for improving the ability to create grammatically correct sentences.

CUSTOMER REVIEW

This is the best app ever for generating language and building concepts. *Language Builder* provides three prompt levels and an optional hint button to support students as they learn the complex structure of language. *Language Builder* can be used in a one-on-one therapy session or a language-building group. I have, quite literally, had students talk more to the app than to me. And the greatest feature *Language Builder* has is the ability to record, store, replay, and easily share (via email) all language accomplishments. My students who prefer not to be recorded have tons of fun listening to and talking about peer recordings. Because *Language Builder* has a simple-to-use record button, I can use it to help students with voice or articulation goals learn to self-monitor and self-correct.

STORYBUILDER

by Mobile Education Tools

http://sites.google.com/site/mobileeducationstore

$3.99

FROM THE DEVELOPER

StoryBuilder is designed to help children accomplish the following educational goals: 1) Improve paragraph formation; 2) Improve integration of ideas; and 3) Improve higher level abstractions by inference. Extensive use of audio clips promotes improved auditory processing for special needs children with autism spectrum disorders or sensory processing disorders.

CUSTOMER REVIEW

If you like mini scenarios and telling short stories, *StoryBuilder* is the app for you. The stories begin with a high-interest picture. The user is then asked a series of questions that is answered verbally via a record button. When the story is complete, simply touch the Play Story button and hear your recordings. Recordings can be sent to family or friends to increase generalization and self esteem. Visual prompts and sentence starters are utilized for every question.

The user does not choose the story. Some stories depend upon imagination and may not be relevant to all users. Recommended for students who have challenges with topic maintenance, abstractions, inferences, verbal sequencing, and coherence.

GUESS 'EM

by GameWeaver

http://guessem.gameweaver.com

FREE

FROM THE DEVELOPER

Guess 'em is a guessing game where you try to find out which face your friend has by asking a series of questions such as "Do they have big eyes?" and "Are they wearing purple?"

CUSTOMER REVIEW

If you like to play "Guess Who?" then you will love Guess'em. This game is meant to be played with two devices; however, it can be easily modified to use with one device. Simply have one student choose a picture, write it down (to remember) and have the second student ask a question to deduce who player one selected. This game is very language rich, gets students interacting and asking questions. *Guess 'em* also targets problem-solving skills and categorization. Three game boards came with my download. All free! Highly recommended as a must-have app for speech-language pathologists.

DESCRIBING WORDS

by The Conover Company

www.conovercompany.com/ipod/apps

$0.99

FROM THE DEVELOPER

The *Describing Words* application is designed to teach and reinforce basic words for functional literacy. *Describing Words* provides easy-to-understand information that allows users to become more capable and to function independently.

CUSTOMER REVIEW

Part of the *Functional Skills System*, *Describing Words* focuses on descriptors. The user is provided with multiple modes of learning for each descriptor. There is a short video that defines the word and uses it in a sentence, along with the correct spelling and pronunciation. The *Functional Skills System* apps are a very well-thought-out and developed set of learning tools. Check them all out. Data tracking is the only additional option that could make *Describing Words* even better for an educator.

GUESS THE ANIMALS

by TapToLearn Software

http://taptolearn.com

$0.99

> **What Animal Am I?**
>
> I am big and very hairy, The "teddy" version of me keeps the night from being scary, I hibernate the winter through, Watching my cubs play cheers you up when you are blue.
>
> Shark
>
> Donkey
>
> Bear

FROM THE DEVELOPER

*Guess the Animal*s is a game for school kids and adults that asks users to guess which animal is being described, based on a set of clues.

CUSTOMER REVIEW

Need practice in making inferences, describing, auditory processing, and auditory memory? Then *Guess the Animal*s is for you. I play the game like 30 Second Mysteries, reading one clue at a time until the correct answer is given. I urge TapToLearn Software to make more versions (Guess the Vehicle, Guess the Occupation). Highly recommended as a recreational learning app.

WORDS—SYNONYMS & ANTONYMS

by Clay Cat Designs

www.claycat.com

$0.99

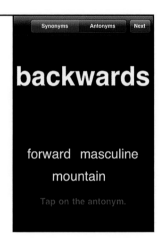

FROM THE DEVELOPER

Practice your knowledge of synonyms and antonyms! An antonym is a word that means the opposite of another word. A synonym is a word with the same or similar meaning as another word.

CUSTOMER REVIEW

Words—Synonyms & Antonyms is for individuals who want to practice or learn either synonyms or anonyms. The user is given a word and three possible solutions to choose from.

 The user cannot search like a dictionary to find a specific synonym or antonym.

WORDS—HOMOPHONES

by Clay Cat Designs

www.claycat.com

$0.99

FROM THE DEVELOPER

The *Words—Homophones* app will help you master commonly used homophones in the English language as well as the meanings of the words. Homophones gives you a sentence and the possible meanings of the homophone used in that sentence. Your task is to choose the correct meaning.

CUSTOMER REVIEW

Homophones and multiple meaning words are abstract, difficult-to-master language concepts. *Words—Homophones* will give the user practice in understanding that, sometimes, words have more than one meaning.

 The user does not have the ability to search for desired words.

IDIOM DICTIONARY

by Deep Powder Software

http://web.me.com/deeppowdersoftware/Deep_Powder_Software/Welcome.html

$1.99

FROM THE DEVELOPER

Our *Idiom Dictionary* application for the iPhone and iPod touch is a Dictionary/Glossary of thousands of great idioms from all over the world. An idiom is an expression, word, or phrase that has a figurative meaning.

CUSTOMER REVIEW

With over 3,000 idioms, *Idiom Dictionary* is a comprehensive reference tool. *Idiom Dictionary* has made it easy to find specific idioms by providing the user with an alphabetical and a keyword search. If you have difficulty understanding figurative language or are struggling to master the subtleties of the English language, *Idiom Dictionary* is for you.

Part IV

Pragmatics & Social Skills

According to the American Speech-Language-Hearing Association (ASHA), an individual may say words clearly and use long, complex sentences with correct grammar, but still have a communication problem if he or she has not mastered the rules of social language known as pragmatics. Pragmatic disorders often coexist with other disabilities and can lower social acceptance. Peers may avoid having conversations with an individual with a pragmatic disorder.

Individuals with pragmatic challenges may say inappropriate things in conversation, be disorganized, have poor personal hygiene, have difficulty reading or displaying body language, and poor eye contact. These impairments are not always obvious to an outsider. Often, individuals with poor pragmatic skills get labled as "weird," or as "geeks." If you think back through your life, I'm sure you can remember those who just didn't fit in. It is my sincere hope that one or all of the folowing apps can help alleviate some of the stigma and heartache that goes along with poor social pragmatic skills.

Chapter 11:
Video Modeling

Video modeling is a highly effective, evidence-based method used in teaching social skills and desired behaviors to individuals on the autism spectrum and those who require visual supports to learn.

Using the iPod to Teach Freedom and Independence

—by Mike Schmitz

We live in an exciting time. Technology is making it easier and easier for people with disabilities to function independently in their homes, workplaces, schools, and communities. Things that were once thought impossible are now possible with the aid of these innovations. Every day there are new tools available to assist in the transition toward independent living, but none have had as big an impact as the iPod touch. When most people think of an iPod, they think of it as a portable music player. The truth is that it is actually an amazingly powerful assistive technology tool, which allows the learner to take instruction out into the community. Using the iPod touch, you can:

- Plan your day
- Follow directions
- Use public transportation
- Perform work activities

- Go to school, work, shopping, etc.

- Create a shopping list

- Go to a restaurant

- Handle difficult social situations

- Much, much more!

The possibilities with the iPod are endless. With the right content, you can use the video and audio abilities of the iPod touch to teach freedom and independence in new ways, and—most importantly—give learners the motivation they need to learn.

THINKING IN PICTURES

The concept of thinking in pictures is nothing new. In fact, The Conover Company has been teaching freedom and independence using this philosophy since 1982. At that time research was very limited on the topic of computer-based software using pictures and audio to teach functional survival skills to youth and adults with significant disabilities, but The Conover Company was in the forefront of that research. We developed a software program called Survival Words. Survival Words taught 60 functional survival skills in a picture format with full audio. The program was targeted for individuals with no reading skills.

We began a process of software development incorporating pictures with various levels of audio, including English and Spanish, to teach basic survival words concepts such as "stop," "go," "caution," etc., all the critical words needed for freedom and independence in our society. The software concept was simple—present the picture along with an audio track saying the targeted word; for example, "Stop." The next step showed the word or sign in context, as it is used in real life, with an audio track describing the situation.

Our design back then was just as valid as it is today. A picture, or better yet, a video, is worth a thousand words. We called this the Instructional Phase. In the Instructional Review we began to bring in distracters, both auditory and visual, to make sure the learner understood the concept. Finally came a Generalization Phase. This phase allowed the sign or the word to be generalized in everyday use in the community.

This basic design worked well for us back in the early days of software development but it had its limitations. For example, each picture had to be hand drawn, one pixel at a time. We used the True Apple Tablet, using a stylus to draw pixelated lines, which required a lot of skill and patience. The audio was recorded and then converted to a poor-quality, robotic-sounding voice. It was crude, but better than anything else at the time, and it was an effective way to teach these important skills.

The first year we released Survival Words, we sold six programs for the Apple II computer. So much for that—or so we thought. Out of the six programs that were sold, two were used for graduate-level research on whether this new computer-based technology could improve upon the traditional, teacher-led format for teaching survival skills. The results were very promising and showed that, yes, students with significant disabilities could and did learn survival skills from a software program if it was designed to accommodate their particular learning needs. More importantly, information learned through this computer format could be easily transferred to the community.

Today, all our programs use digital pictures, video, and human-quality audio. The video format takes the "thinking in pictures" concept to a whole new level, and with the advancements in digital video we are able to move to more complex activities. This led to the development of our How To Series. The How To Series uses the same instructional format as our Signs and Words Series to teach basic activities requiring a variety of sequenced steps, such as crossing the street or brushing your teeth.

As we developed these programs we continued to shoot thousands of short video clips—video clips that are now used in our iPod applications to reinforce these crucial independent living skills. We now have more than 3,500 video clips in our Functional Skills System. This series now includes 42 programs covering functional life and social skills, literacy, math, and work skills, with more programs under development.

MOTIVATION TO LEARN

Many research studies have been conducted since our original Survival Words program was released over 25 years ago for the Apple II, and studies were done on the effects of computer-based instruction for individuals who have significant learning difficulties. Many theories have been presented about the effects of computer-based instruction for teaching functional life and social skills, literacy, work, and math skills. When you boil all of that research down it points to one single element that is the most important factor in this large body of research. This factor is motivation. Learners with special needs are no different than any other learners in this regard. The desire to learn new skills is fueled by motivation, and this motivation makes learners with special needs appear no different from anyone else in our society. Correctly-designed computer software provides individuals with an opportunity to learn like everyone else.

I will never forget the beginning of the software revolution in education. In those days, classrooms seldom had computers for special needs students so it was necessary to carry a computer into the school and set it up in order to do a demonstration. When it came time for me to leave and carry the equipment back out, I never lacked for volunteers to assist me. It did not take long to realize that these students wanted to be seen in the hallways carrying that Apple II computer.

This early computer revolution has evolved to the iPod revolution of today. Motivation to learn is dramatically enhanced when these skills are reinforced on the iPod. Learners with special needs WANT to be seen carrying an iPod, because they desire to be like everyone else. The iPod itself is a "cool" tool for learning, and the best thing about the iPod is that it is small, portable, and fits easily in your pocket.

In the last few months, we at The Conover Company have launched a movement which has taken the industry by storm. We have taken all 42 of our Functional Skills System software programs and created iPod applications for each program. (You can download our apps from the iTunes App Store. Simply search for "conover" and you will find them.)

GETTING PARENTS INVOLVED

Perhaps one of the most exciting advantages of our iPod applications is that parents can now be involved in their sons' and daughters' education process. Our apps are currently selling for 99¢ each—less than a cup of coffee. These very affordable applications are a great way to review at home what's being taught at school, because parents can now access the same technology that we make available in the schools. The apps are easy to use with our unique user interface, provide direct access to any of the videos in the application, and can be used over and over again.

While the apps do not have all of the functionality of our Functional Skills System software, they do include all the videos from their software counterparts—approximately 80 video clips in each app. With the use of these applications, there is no longer a disconnect between what is being taught in school and what is being reinforced at home. The tools available to parents today will enable parents to help their sons or daughters learn these key life and social skills, literacy, math, and work skills essential to function more independently in their homes, workplaces, schools, and communities.

See for yourself how The Conover Company's iPod applications can make learning new skills fun while making a dramatic difference in the lives of your children.

Success Story: Alex

Alex is a handsome, 12-year-old boy with autism. His verbal language consists of echolalia, ritualistic speech, and unintelligible lines from movies and TV. Alex can read at the Kindergarten level. He memorizes certain rhythmic books and may repeat lines at inappropriate times. Alex likes social attention; however, he does not know how to get it in a positive manner. Alex instantly took to the iPod touch, like a fish to water.

His first app was *Model Me Going Places* by Model Me Kids, LLC. He would read all the social stories and look for more. In a few weeks we began hearing phrases from the social stories make their way to his language. After social stories he began to play *First Words Animals*. In this app there is spelling and vocabulary development. Now, Alex can spell and label all the animals on this app. He will occasionally draw on *Doodle Buddy* and is fascinated by *iHourglass*. Alex flipped when I first introduced the iPad. He will now complete his classroom goals and earn tokens for time on the iPad. Just today, he began sharing his time with a friend and taking turns. *Proloquo2Go* is next followed by *Speak it!* Mom and Dad are going to buy Alex his own iPad soon. Great work, Alex!

FUNCTIONAL SKILLS SYSTEM (42 APPS)

by The Conover Company

www.conovercompany.com/ipod/apps

- Functional Life Skills (19 Apps)
- Functional Literacy Skills (7 Apps)
- Functional Social Skills (6 Apps)
- Functional Work Skills (3 Apps)
- Functional Math Skills (3 Apps)
- Functional Skills Sampler (4 Apps)

All are $0.99 each, but the Sampler is FREE

FROM THE DEVELOPER

For some, going on a shopping trip, using basic literacy skills, understanding what to do when seeing a warning sign, or transitioning from school to work, are very difficult tasks. The *Functional Skills System* software provides easy-to-understand information that allows learners to become more capable of functioning independently in their homes, schools, communities, and workplaces. This system increases a learner's ability to make appropriate choices. Gaining functional literacy, social, life, and work skills allows for freedom and independence. These programs are for anyone trying to become more functionally independent in our society.

 Conover Company will be releasing a Shopping List generator, a Daily Activity List generator and a Communication tool shortly.

FUNCTIONAL SKILLS SYSTEM (continued)

CUSTOMER REVIEW

Finally, I can take social skills into the community where they belong and practice in real time and in natural situations. Video modeling has proven to be a fast, effective training method for teaching tasks to individuals with autism and those who require visual supports for success. Students on the spectrum are often unable to absorb information or maintain attention through a one-on-one, or classroom demonstration. *Functional Skills Sampler* provides individuals on the spectrum the visual support they need to practice a skill until it is mastered. And now it is easy to practice at home, school, and with parents and educators to encourage generalization and success.

MODEL ME GOING PLACES

by Model Me Kids, LLC

www.modelmekids.com

FREE

FROM THE DEVELOPER

Model Me Going Places™ is a great visual teaching tool for helping your child learn to navigate challenging locations in the community. Each location contains a photo slide show of children modeling appropriate behavior. Locations include:

- Doctor
- Playground
- Hairdresser

- Mall
- Restaurant
- Grocery Store

CUSTOMER REVIEW

This app is so important to all students on the spectrum. *Model Me Going Places* features six functional social stories. The stories are read in book style with music in the background. My students watch these stories over and over again. Students with a limited ability to talk read along with *Model Me Going Places*. They read along and eventually begin using the language in their daily lives. The narration could be more articulate. Some of the words are difficult to understand without the graphics to support meaning. Be that as it may, I liked it so much, I bought the DVD collection. Sometimes the best things in life are free!

SMALLTALK APHASIA & SMALLTALK COMMON PHRASES

by Lingraphica

www.aphasia.com

FREE

FROM THE DEVELOPER

SmallTalk Common Phrases and *SmallTalk Aphasia* apps provide a series of speech-exercise videos, each illustrating the tongue and lip movements necessary to produce a commonly used short phrase in everyday vocabulary. With this app, people with apraxia, aphasia, and/or dysarthria resulting from stroke or head injury can easily practice commonly used phrases and repeat each one as often as they like.

CUSTOMER REVIEW

The SmallTalk app series is excellent! I have searched for video clips of the articulators for many years. Both *SmallTalk Common Phrases* and *SmallTalk Aphasia* provide the user with clear audio, graphics, text, and video of common phrases. *SmallTalk Aphasia* has an additional icons feature, which provides common phrases in written and graphic form. The SmallTalk series was originally meant for adults with aphasia; however, they work fabulously with students on the spectrum and/or students with apraxia. SmallTalk apps provide video modeling for speech. I would also like to note that. an iPad, iPod touch, or iPhone are superb companions and time killers for individuals in the hospital. Now, these same iDevices can also communicate important medical information. I highly recommended SmallTalk apps for individuals with apraxia, aphasia, dysarthria, and autism of all ages.

SMALLTALK LETTERS, NUMBERS, COLORS

by Lingraphica

www.aphasia.com

FREE

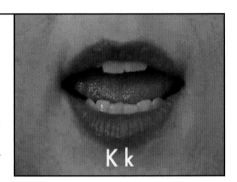

FROM THE DEVELOPER

The *SmallTalk Letters, Numbers, Colors* app provides a series of speech-exercise videos, each illustrating the tongue and lip movements necessary to produce a single color, number, or letter. With this app, people with apraxia, aphasia, and/or dysarthria resulting from stroke or head injury can easily practice individual colors, numbers, or letters as often as they like.

CUSTOMER REVIEW

SmallTalk Letters, Numbers, Colors was developed to help folks who have had strokes or head injury practice tongue and lip movements to produce single words. My colleagues in the hospitals tell me that SmallTalk apps work incredibly well with those scenarios. I use *Letters, Numbers, Colors* with my students on the spectrum and/or with apraxia and they work equally fabulously. One young man was so excited by the video modeling he spent a whole afternoon filing through letters, numbers, and colors until it was time to go home. The next session, he began repeating after the video model. Success. Recommended for anyone who has apraxia, motor planning challenges, or depends upon visual input for success.

Chapter 12: Social Skills Group Activities

S ocial groups are intended to build social interaction techniques to provide individuals with an array of skills from basic conversations, sharing, practicing nonverbal language and eye-contact, to complex and subtle skills like relationships and dating.

iTAKE TURNS

by Smarty Ears

www.smarty-ears.com

$1.99

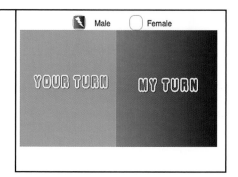

FROM THE DEVELOPER

Taking turns can be very difficult for young children with disabilities. *iTake Turns* makes teaching turn-taking a lot more fun!

CUSTOMER REVIEW

iTake Turns is super simple. When playing a two-person game, the users can indicate who's turn it is by selecting the, "my turn" or "your turn" button. The cool thing about this is, after several rounds, the students begin to repeat the words, "my turn" and "your turn." That is worth the higher price. Users also have the choice of a male or female voice. The cartoon voice from the *Answers: YesNo* app would have been a nice option.

SOCIAL SKILLS

by MDR

www.*look2learn*.com/*look2learn*

$6.99

"My turn." The girl raises her hand.

FROM THE DEVELOPER

Social Skills (S2L) offers parents and educators the ability to interact with six social narratives, broken into two levels providing a total possible of 12 social narratives, designed to help individuals improve their social ability. With *Social Skills (S2L)*, the stories contain targeted instruction in the following core areas: joint attention, nonverbal communication, greetings, structured game play, turn-taking, classroom rules, and imitation.

CUSTOMER REVIEW

Given the ability to customize over 100 photos with audio and text, *Social Skills* can target individualized social skills. *Social Skills* comes with six stories that are divided into basic and advanced levels, thus offering educators, parents, and caregivers the ability to pinpoint and build upon acquired skills. In addition, users can customize pictures and audio for even more flexibility. Recommended as a multi-modality tool to enhance social skills in the school environment and beyond.

iTOPICS—CONVERSATION STARTERS

by Opticalistic

http://opticalistic.com

$0.99

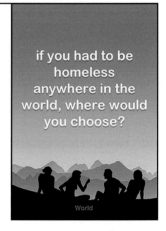

if you had to be homeless anywhere in the world, where would you choose?

World

FROM THE DEVELOPER

iTopics–Conversation Starters are open-ended and designed to elicit further conversation, touching on such loaded topics as morality, memories of youth, the future, and more.

CUSTOMER REVIEW

Starting and maintaining a conversation can be nerve-racking for some individuals. *iTopics* is an excellent way to practice initiating a conversation and engaging others. The skills necessary for dialogue with others often elude individuals on the spectrum. *iTopics* is helpful in starting and maintaining conversations, and eventually making friends. It would be nice if *iTopics* included some basic rules of conversation within their app. Here is a quick list:

- Eye contact is important
- Arm's length is appropriate conversation distance
- Express emotion by varying the tone of voice
- Stay on topic
- Let others change the subject
- Ask questions and remember a person's likes and dislikes
- Respond to questions being asked
- Take turns in conversation
- Practice listening skills

BRAINPOP FEATURED MOVIE

by BrainPOP

www.brainpop.com/apps/about

FREE

FROM THE DEVELOPER

Learn something different each day with the free *BrainPOP Featured Movie* app for the iPad, iPhone, and iPod touch! After watching *BrainPOP*'s daily animated movie, you can test your new knowledge with an interactive quiz.

CUSTOMER REVIEW

I have used *BrainPOP* in many different educational frameworks. Sometimes I use it just to get information, usually topical. I also use it in social group settings for topic maintenance. My favorite use is to have one student review the featured movie de jour and then lead the others in a discussion. *BrainPOP*, please add a movie library!

YOU MUST CHOOSE!

by Indigo Penguin Limited

website currently unavailable

FREE

You Must Choose! is like the board game, Would You Rather?, in an app. It is rated "E" for

Everyone.

CUSTOMER REVIEW

The questions in *You Must Choose!* are simple, yet make you think about your answer.

Students can answer the questions for themselves or predict what another might choose

and why. Here are some examples of the thought provoking questions you may get asked.

You Must Choose:

- Be a superhero? Or be a supervillain?

- Eat a hairy pizza? Or eat a saliva sandwich?

- One wish granted today? Or five wishes granted in three

  years' time?

I use the *You Must Choose!* in social pragmatic groups to encourage peer interaction,

topic maintenance, and turn-taking. Because it is a motivating game to play, I have good

participation and cooperation. The spinning choice wheel and advertisements I could do

without.

WAY NO WAY™: AMAZING FACTS

by Spinapse, Inc.

http://spinapse.com/details.html?id=1015

$0.99

FROM THE DEVELOPER

Way No Way is a new trivia game with a twist ... and a spin ... and a truckload of facts that we cooked up fresh, not from a can. We worked hard to make sure that the trivia is 100% true and the game play will make your heart race, with minimal risk of long-term damage.

CUSTOMER REVIEW

Way No Way is the perfect app for a social group. Students take turns, maintain topics, and learn interesting facts at the same time. Up to five single players can be entered into profiles or the game can be played in teams. The first player spins to determine points. Then you are asked a quirky trivia question that you answer by touching the "Way" or "No Way" button. Instantly the game provides feedback and additional information about the question. *Way No Way* also provides users with a scoring system that lets you compare your scores locally or worldwide. Pretty cool for 99 cents!

MR. TRIVIA

by Iron Square

www.iron-square.com

$1.99

FROM THE DEVELOPER

It's *Mr. Trivia*! This casual trivia game features more than 2,000 questions presented to you in a classic, quirky, '50s game style.

CUSTOMER REVIEW

Mr. Trivia is a jocular game that can be used for social groups, turn-taking and topic maintenance skills. *Mr. Trivia* features 2,000 lighthearted trivia questions, seven categories, a "lightning round," and virtual prizes. Individuals can play as a group, in teams, or take turns being the host. If you are not sure that *Mr. Trivia* is right for you, try the free version first.

WARNING! May cause extreme cockiness!

ESTEEM AID

by Wet Leaf Software

www.wetleafsoftware.com

$0.99

You are AWESOME!!

Shake for new message.

FROM THE DEVELOPER

Welcome to *Esteem Aid*, the program that recognizes some of us just need a shot in the arm to get us going. Get the praise you deserve any time of the day. After all, who needs a lot of friends when *Esteem Aid* is only a pocket away?

CUSTOMER REVIEW

Esteem Aid is here to save the day for those of us who occasionally suffer from low self-esteem. One user called this app "cheesy." I would have to agree; however, the fact is that many individuals with disabilities suffer from low self-esteem. Although "cheesy," it puts a smile on faces and encourages a better attitude. I like it.

 There is no audio, so the user should have some reading skills.

CHOW CHAT

by Shoe The Goose

www.shoethegoose.com

$0.99

FROM THE DEVELOPER

Chow Chat is an engaging, educational app that brings the family closer while encouraging critical thinking, language development, and the sharing of diverse ideas.

CUSTOMER REVIEW

What a great way to spark imagination while learning something about your friends and family! *Chow Chat* provides thought-provoking facts, quotes, and proverbs followed by related questions to encourage individuals to share thoughts, ideas, and opinions. I use *Chow Chat* for social groups to encourage topic maintenance, conversations, and friendships. *Chow Chat* is excellent practice for anyone who has difficulty initiating and maintaining social interactions. Users have the ability to edit pre-existing information or add their own facts, thoughts, and proverbs. Rating and grouping settings help keep all facts organized for easy access. All material is rated "E" for everyone.

QUIZZLER DATING

by Perkel Communications

www.pcommapps.com

$0.99

FROM THE DEVELOPER

Quizzler Dating is the question game that breaks the ice by acting as an immediate conversation starter. Thought-provoking, funny, yet simple, questions stimulate insightful answers that help you learn about someone quickly and figure out if you're a good match.

CUSTOMER REVIEW

Quizzler Dating will help break the ice on a first date, start a conversation, or just get acquainted with another human. With *Quizzler* you can customize your own questions, create a "favorites" play list, or choose to answer all the questions randomly. Recommended for getting to know someone. Rated "E" for everyone.

QUIZZLER FAMILY

by Perkel Communications

www.pcommapps.com

$0.99

FROM THE DEVELOPER

Quizzler Family is the fun question game that turns "down time" into "quality time" as everyone answers fun, insightful, and silly questions.

CUSTOMER REVIEW

Start a conversation anytime, anywhere, or just get to know someone better with the help of *Quizzler Family*. Social skills groups are a breeze with this app and educators do not have to worry about inappropriate questions. *Quizzler Family* questions are also great story starters for written assignments.

Chapter 13: Eye Contact & Body Language

Body language is the second form of communication that humans use to express themselves. An individual with autism has difficulty deciphering what a person is saying through facial expressions or body language. Most people with autism also have a hard time making eye contact. They appear to be in a world that is centered in themselves and the nuances of a gesture or facial expression are lost. Visual supports and practice, practice, practice can help individuals navigate through the confusing world of facial expressions and body language.

EYE CONTACT-TOYBOX &
LOOK IN MY EYES—RESTAURANT

by FizzBrain

www.fizzbrain.com

$2.99 each

FROM THE DEVELOPER

Eye contact is an important social skill that some children find challenging. *Eye Contact–Toybox* and *Look in My Eyes–Restaurant* help them practice this skill, while earning fun rewards and playing creatively. These apps were designed for children on the autism spectrum—especially those with Asperger's syndrome—but any child who has difficulties with eye contact may benefit from playing.

CUSTOMER REVIEW

Look In My Eyes–Restaurant is a helpful app to encourage generalization of eye contact. Recommended for higher functioning or Asperger's students. I have had parents tell me that their child was averse to this app at first, but was lured in with earning rewards.

    Eye Contact–Toybox is similar to the *Look In My Eyes* app, only easier. It is recommended for slightly younger students. Both are good at encouraging eye contact and imagination. Students with more severe deficits will not attend or understand the task. Both apps require the user to look into the eyes of a series of faces to discover the correct answers to number-based questions. Users can earn rewards for correct answers.

 Both apps are engaging, but not to all.

SMILE AT ME

by FizzBrain

www.fizzbrain.com

$2.99

FROM THE DEVELOPER

Is smiling an issue for your child? *Smile at Me* is an engaging way to practice this social skill in a safe setting—with fun rewards!

CUSTOMER REVIEW

Many individuals on the spectrum have difficulty with interpreting and displaying facial expression. *Smile at Me* is a delightful way to practice the most basic facial expressions of smiling and frowning. The student is shown a picture that will elicit a smile or frown and is encouraged to hold the iDevice like a mirror (to see their reflection in the glass) and to compare their mouth to that of the child in the picture. The picture on the app dims every few seconds to allow the student to view his own facial expression and practice making smiles or frowns with the pictures. The student then decides if the child in the picture is smiling or frowning and touches the corresponding image. If correct, the student earns a star. After the child has earned four stars, a virtual trip to the zoo is earned, where more social skills are practiced and generalized. The developers of *Smile at Me* make no promises that practicing this game will affect real behavior; however, they do believe that smiling is a cultural norm that can be learned with practice.

MICRO-EXPRESSION TRAINER

by Mario Micklisch

http://favo.asia/2010/03/micro-expression-trainer

$3.99

FROM THE DEVELOPER

Many individuals on the spectrum have difficulty reading and expressing emotions. *Micro-Expression Trainer* can help individuals by showing what an emotion looks like and describing the facial features that accompany the expression. *Micro-Expression Trainer* expresses the seven universal emotions—anger, contempt, disgust, fear, happiness, sadness, and surprise—that are brief, involuntary facial expressions shown on the face in response to the emotions someone is experiencing.

CUSTOMER REVIEW

By having both the written explanation and the visual input, with *Micro-Expression Trainer*, individuals can practice (using a mirror) making these expressions themselves. There is no audio or sound effects, only beautiful faces making expressions.

 To repeat the facial expression you have to tap the small circle-arrow in the bottom right corner. I thought you would tap the face for a repetition. I have found that Micro-Expression Trainer is also good for encouraging eye contact as the user must look at the face for approximately five seconds to see the entire expression loop when the duration is set to maximum.

AUTISMXPRESS

by StudioEmotion Pty Ltd. Inc.

http://autismspectrum.org.au/iPhone

FREE

FROM THE DEVELOPER

The *AutismXpress* iPhone app has been created to help promote greater awareness about autism spectrum disorders. It is designed to encourage people with autism to recognize and express their emotions through its fun and easy-to-use interface.

CUSTOMER REVIEW

Hilarious, silly, and free. My students really like *AutismXpress*. The facial animations and sounds are really fun. *AutismXpress* features 12 faces with common feelings. Choose one and see the delightful animation and sound effect that accompanies the feeling. Perfect for the, "How are you doing?" segment of circle time. "Gassy" is a favorite among the boys. I recommend *AutismXpress* for all students as a learning tool or reinforcer.

BODYLANGUAGE

by Wolfgang Horbach

www.sabine-muehlisch.de/*bodylanguage*-iPhone-app/

bodylanguage-iPhone-app-en

$0.99

FROM THE DEVELOPER

What's your body language saying about you? Are you exuding a confident, relaxed attitude or are your tense insecurities showing? You can't hide how you're really feeling; it shows in the way you move, speak, stand, and carry yourself. With *BodyLanguage*, put a personal coach in your iPhone and improve your body language and outlook.

CUSTOMER REVIEW

BodyLanguage is a self-help app that was originally meant for the business world to guide the user through meetings, presentations, and appointments. I use it to bring awareness and confidence to my students who have difficulty acknowledging and using body language. *BodyLanguage* will guide you through everyday interactions by giving details on gestures, greetings, and keeping it cool.

 $0.99 is just the beginning. If you want all the information, you will have to purchase six more apps from $0.99 to $3.99. Even though *BodyLanguage* is rather stiff and business-like, I do recommend it for individuals wanting to improve their nonverbal communication skills.

MAGIC EYEBALL

by Joy Entertainment LLC

http://joyentertainmentllc.com/Joy_Entertainment_LLC

$0.99

FROM THE DEVELOPER

Consult the all-knowing, all-seeing mystical eye and all your questions will be answered! Take a deep breath, ask a question, and press the pupil. It will blink and give you your answer. Press the pupil again and it will blink and you can ask another question. Very simple, yet very powerful.

CUSTOMER REVIEW

Just like the "Magic 8 Ball," *Magic Eyeball* inspires question-asking and social interaction as well as eye contact. Just ask a yes/no question, tap the eye, and get the answer. When the *Magic Eyeball* is not answering questions, the eye follows the user from side to side—kinda creepy! *Magic Eyeball* has been responsible for some lively social groups. Did I mention that *Magic Eyeball* encourages eye contact?

Chapter 14: Hygiene & Pre-Vocational

Even though adulthood may seem far away or may be just around the corner, it is never too late or early to work on independent life skills, pre-vocational, and self care. There are things everyone can do and starting early is the key to success.

A recent study from Australia, "iPod Therefore I Can: Enhancing the Learning of Children with Intellectual Disabilities through Emerging Technologies," tracked the progress of ten autistic children who were using iPod touches. Results indicate that corrective behavior was reinforced in children with autism who, in one case, couldn't wash their hands, by combining images and voiceover. An amazing 60% of the study's goals were achieved.

Success Story: Earl

Earl is a very interesting teenage boy. He is able to spell, follow multi-step directions, and communicate well via picture exchange. Yet he is unable to talk. He is a full-size young man who has intense likes and dislikes. Family members have warned the staff about Earl's dislike for brushing his teeth. As a matter of fact, Earl's Grandpa is the only person Earl allows to brush his teeth. This year at Earl's IEP his family was deeply concerned about his oral hygiene as Grandpa had fallen ill.

The occupational therapist and I took it upon ourselves to support Earl with his goal of independent oral hygiene. After lunch, we demonstrated brushing teeth with the *iBrush* app and had Earl practice. After that we walked him to the sink, gave him a toothbrush and toothpaste, showed him the app again, and with hand-over-hand prompts brushed his teeth. The next day, he required set up and some verbal prompts, with review of the app. By the third day, we switched apps to *Brush Teeth* (for generalization), set him up, and he completed the task. Earl needed to see why brushing was important. *iBrush* and *Brush Teeth* gave him the visual support needed to understand the task. Goal Met!

iBRUSH

by JAGLABS, Inc.

www.imindsoftware.com

FREE

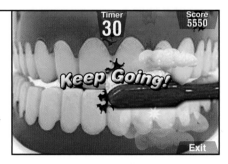

FROM THE DEVELOPER

iBrush is a fun new way to help teach young (and maybe not so young) children how to keep that fantastic smile, and make the world just a little bit brighter.

CUSTOMER REVIEW

Sure enough, there's an app for that. *iBrush* seems like a novelty app, yet, it has proven to be terrific in giving students on the autism spectrum the visual input they need to support good oral hygiene. Once they have completed the task on the app and we have had a few giggles, students feel more confident putting the toothbrush into their mouths. Please read Earl's success story (above) to get a better understanding of the power of visual supports. Included in this app is information on how to best get teeth clean, how often to brush teeth, how regularly to change toothbrushes, and even prompts for flossing (that's another app).

 It is super difficult to get the teeth totally clean. This can be frustrating, usually only to the adults facilitating the *iBrush* challenge.

BRUSH TEETH FREE

by Runic

www.runicdev.com

$0.99

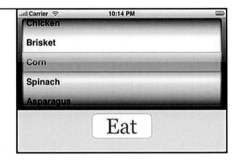

FROM THE DEVELOPER

Love brushing teeth? Who doesn't? HILARIOUS app!

CUSTOMER REVIEW

Brush Teeth Free is fantastic for giving individuals the visual support they need to understand why brushing your teeth is important. The user chooses the food item to be brushed away, touches the eat button and then uses their finger to clean teeth.

 There is no audio or graphic toothbrush with this app.

iDRESS FOR WEATHER

by Pebro Productions

www.pebroproductions.com/iDress_for_Weather.html

$1.99

FROM THE DEVELOPER

Unlike other weather apps that have too much unattractive

clutter, *iDress for Weather* provides only the images and weather

conditions that are essential for daily use. And unlike any other

weather app, *iDress for Weather* provides a customizable closet

that can contain clothes matching the weather conditions for

that day: use the current illustrations or personalize with your own photos or images!

CUSTOMER REVIEW

Up-to-date weather information with a full set of clothing suggestions at the swipe of a

finger: *iDress for Weather* offers concrete information for those individuals who have diffi-

culty matching clothing and accessories to the daily weather conditions. Parents now have

visual support to reinforce the connection between weather and clothing for their children.

Parents and caregivers can also customize the closet contents. Simply snap a picture of the

clothing that goes with a weather condition and add it to the corresponding closet. The

ability to configure temperature ranges to personal preferences, and the opportunity to

customize extended info like humidity, wind, location and units of measure (Fahrenheit or

Celsius) are choices provided in the settings. *iDress for Weather* is fantastic for supporting

individuals in making appropriate clothing choices for the day.

DRESS ME UP

by Captive Games

http://rockislandgames.com/index.php?iPhone

$0.99

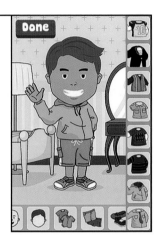

FROM THE DEVELOPER

Create a character selecting different faces and hair styles. Then add clothes: tops, bottoms, shoes, hats, and accessories. Choose a background and you've created your own custom character. Lots of different combinations for kids to try!

CUSTOMER REVIEW

What should I wear today? *Dress Me Up* can help individuals make appropriate clothing choices by providing visual input. The user selects a background (location) and dresses the character to suit the setting. Choices are given for tops, bottoms, shoes, accessories, glasses, hair, facial expression, and skin color. The only missing feature is weather-related choices, important to individuals on the spectrum. In addition, *Dress Me Up* is a superb app for labeling and increasing use of descriptors (people, places, and things). *Dress Me Up* offers a free trial version of all their apps.

SANTAWEATHER & WHAT2WEAR

by Syargey Kundevich

http://obama-weather.com

$0.99 (*SantaWeather*)

$1.99 (*what2wear*)

FROM THE DEVELOPER

SantaWeather and *what2wear* summons a detailed weather report, analyzes a relation of temperature, humidity, strength of wind, and some other characteristics and, finally, Santa visualizes the most comfortable set of clothes to wear this day.

CUSTOMER REVIEW

Many of my students find it difficult to dress appropriately for the weather. *SantaWeather* is a unique way to help decide what to wear. We frequently use the phrase, "What would Santa wear?" to help make and discuss good clothing choices.

A Wifi connection is needed to use this app. The user can customize units of measurement and locations. If more input is needed for what to wear based on the weather, check out *what2wear*.

iSIGNS HD–150+ COOL SIGNS

by Laan Labs

http://labs.laan.com/wp/products/isigns-hd-150-cool-signs

FREE

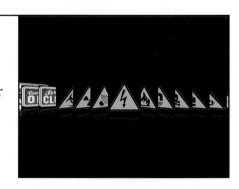

FROM THE DEVELOPER

There's a sign for that! Learning safety signs has never been so much fun with *iSigns HD–150+ Cool Signs*! For fun or business, *iSigns HD* is the answer.

CUSTOMER REVIEW

I had no idea there were so many signs in the environment. Luckily, there is a quick search bar to let the user find the sign(s) they want.

 The signs have no written interpretation, so the user may not know what the sign is for. For example, the logo for *iSigns HD* is a jagged arrow pointing down; I really do not have any idea what that means. Fortunately, most sign meanings are obvious. *iSigns HD* features over 150 beautiful, clear signs that are easy to navigate. Best of all, it's free.

WHAT'S THE RIGHT CAREER FOR YOU?

by Trippert Labs

www.trippertlabs.com

FREE

FROM THE DEVELOPER

Uncertain about the future? Haven't figured out what you're meant to do with your career? Then take this fun quiz and find out the profession that best matches your personality. Remember, for entertainment purposes only. Enjoy!

CUSTOMER REVIEW

What's the Right Career for You? will open up a discussion into careers and personalities. The user answers a set of ten questions and a career option is suggested based on the answers. I have used the questions productively to discuss career opportunities and how they may or may not fit into individual personality types.

 As the developer points out, this app is for entertainment only. Expect lots of ads; they are free too!

FUNCTIONAL SKILLS SYSTEM (42 APPS)

by The Conover Company

www.conovercompany.com/ipod/apps

- Functional Life Skills (19 Apps)
- Functional Literacy Skills (7 Apps)
- Functional Social Skills (6 Apps)
- Functional Work Skills (3 Apps)
- Functional Math Skills (3 Apps)
- Functional Skills Sampler (4 Apps)

All are $0.99 each, but the Sampler is FREE

FROM THE DEVELOPER

For some, going on a shopping trip, using basic literacy skills, understanding what to do when seeing a warning sign, or transitioning from school to work, are very difficult tasks. The *Functional Skills System* software provides easy-to-understand information that allows learners to become more capable of functioning independently in their homes, schools, communities, and workplaces. This system increases a learner's ability to make appropriate choices. Gaining functional literacy, social, life, and work skills allows for freedom and independence. These programs are for anyone trying to become more functionally independent in our society.

 Conover Company will be releasing a Shopping List generator, a Daily Activity List generator and a Communication tool shortly.

FUNCTIONAL SKILLS SYSTEM (continued)

CUSTOMER REVIEW

Finally, I can take social skills into the community where they belong and practice in real time and in natural situations. Video modeling has proven to be a fast, effective training method for teaching tasks to individuals with autism and those who require visual supports for success. Students on the spectrum are often unable to absorb information or maintain attention through a one-on-one, or classroom demonstration. *Functional Skills Sampler* provides individuals on the spectrum the visual support they need to practice a skill until it is mastered. And now it is easy to practice at home, school, and with parents and educators to encourage generalization and success.

Part V

Organizers & Visual, Graphic, & Auditory Aids

Every individual has a unique style of learning. For some, learning comes easily through traditional methods. Others have challenges and need to use different techniques to access information. A highly effective technique used for the visual learner is the use of graphic organizers. Studies have shown that using graphic organizers can help to improve recall, cut down on boredom, stimulate interest, organize thoughts, and enhance understanding of subject matter. Graphic organizers such as storyboards, mind maps, contingency maps, charts, schedules, etc., are traditionally assembled with Velcro, lamination, cardboard, and/or contact paper and then placed in obvious locations so that the user can refer to them throughout their day.

With advancements in technology, graphic organizers and supports can be made in minutes, personalized, taken to any location easily in a pocket or purse, and shared with family (via email). Really! It is just that easy to provide your child/student with the supports they need to cope with each day, feel secure and, in many ways, proud.

Chapter 15: Graphic Organizers & Visual Supports

No longer are visual supports a major construction project of expensive Boardmaker PECs, sticky Velcro, lamination, or contact paper. Nowadays, visual supports are inexpensive, convenient, personalized, and a cinch to make. Here are some of my favorite tried-and-true apps to support the visual learner.

iCOMMUNICATE

by Grembe Inc.

www.grembe.com

$34.99

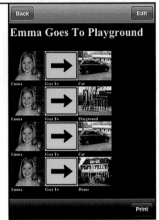

FROM THE DEVELOPER

iCommunicate is a versatile app that will help typically developing children, as well as children with developmental delays and autism. Create pictures, flashcards, storyboards, routines, and visual schedules. Record custom audio in any language. We include 100+ pictures (the first five have audio) to get you started. Add pictures with your camera, or from your camera roll, or use Google image search. Utilize as an audio-visual prompting tool or AAC device.

Jeff Grembe of Grembe Apps would like you to know, "The use of the iPhone/iPod is a revolutionary new platform that will change the lives of people with special needs for the better. We love being a part of this and truly hope these apps make life with your children a little easier!"

CUSTOMER REVIEW

iCommunicate makes storyboards, schedules, menus, and voice output effortless and is a breeze to customize. If familiar with the app, it could take only a few minutes to create a wonderful portable storyboard, choice-board, visual schedule, flashcards, or talking picture album. Visual supports can be printed via iOS 4.2. *iCommunicate* offers a Google image search feature that makes finding great images a snap, plus the option of using

10,000+ SymbolStix images. I remember cutting, laminating, and Velcroing well into the evening. I have heard some grumbling about the programming learning curve, but stick with it; this app is well worth it. Parents have purchased iPads just to use this app with their child.

 iCommunicate was designed to be customized for your individual needs.

POPPLET

by Notion

www.popplet.com

$4.99

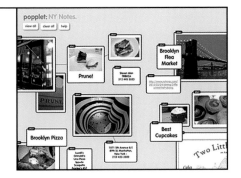

FROM THE DEVELOPER

With *Popplet* you can capture your ideas, sort them visually, and collaborate with others in real time—quickly and easily! You can also sign up for an online account to work on your *popplet*s from your desktop.

CUSTOMER REVIEW

Visual supports are extremely important in the daily lives of individuals on the autism spectrum and *Popplet* is an impressive piece of software that gives life to photo albums, maps, charts, schedules, boards, and more. What is a *popplet*? A *popplet* is like a corkboard or bulletin board on your iDevice that allows users to organize and visually create their ideas. The developers have made it super easy to add pictures (from camera roll), change colors, add text, or draw your own illustration. I have used *Popplet* to build visual supports for just about everything from first-then schedules to complex outlines and essays. Start out by trying the free version to get an idea of how easy *Popplet* is to make use of. The only option that would make *Popplet* more versatile is an Internet image search (hint, hint).

PICTELLO

by AssistiveWare

www.assistiveware.com/*pictello*.php

$14.99

FROM THE DEVELOPER

Pictello is a simple way to create talking photo albums and talking books. Each page in a *Pictello* story can contain a picture, up to five lines of text, and a recorded sound or text-to-speech element using high-quality voices.

CUSTOMER REVIEW

Now, here is a useful alternative to photo albums. *Pictello* is an exceptional app that allows users to capture outings, personalize social stories, create talking books, and share interests and memories with others. Students can create stories at school to share with family members or create stories at home to share with friends at school. *Pictello* comes with a choice of male or female voice and an available child's voice to download free. A record option allows users to personalize adventures using their own voices. Other settings include Expert or Wizard mode. Expert mode allows everyone to easily use the sound and pictures that create personalized stories to share. Wizard mode allows for more creativity with voice and transitions.

 Sharing stories requires both the sender and receiver to have *Pictello* installed on their iDevice.

iPROMPTS®

by Handhold Adaptive, LLC

www.splaysoft.com

$49.99

iPrompts®, the original picture-based prompting app for the iPhone, iPod touch and iPad, is used by parents, special educators, and therapists with developmentally challenged and language-impaired individuals, like people with autism, Down syndrome, Fragile X syndrome, and apraxia. *iPrompts®* also works great with kids who just need more structure, including kids with Attention Deficit Disorder (ADD) and even typical, pre-verbal toddlers! Ten percent of all *iPrompts®* sales now benefit Autism Speaks™.

CUSTOMER REVIEW

This is a great tool to have at your fingertips for portable visual scheduling, choice making, and transitions. I can create schedules on the spot with familiar pictures or choose from a picture library or Web-enabled search. I love the visual countdown timer for transitions. This app was originally designed for younger children; however, I hear the developers are working to make it more teen-friendly.

 iPrompts does not have audio prompts or voice output at this time.

Susan L., SLP/ATC writes, "By using the *iPrompts*, I am able to bypass the printing, cutting, laminating, and storing the material in a workable area. I am recommending this program to my teams as an alternative to the endless paper creation of visual prompts."

Linda M., special education paraprofessional concurs: "I've been dreaming of a day when this software would be made available, after creating hundreds of PECS pictures by hand only to have them lost. This new technology will give hope to many families who have been through so much heartache. Thanks to Handhold Adaptive for creating software that will build a better world!

Evan checks his Picture Schedule

with the help of iPrompts

STRIP DESIGNER

by Vivid Apps

www.mexircus.com/Strip_Designer

$2.99

FROM THE DEVELOPER

With *Strip Designer*, you can create your own personal comic book strips using photos from your photo album or iPhone camera.

CUSTOMER REVIEW

Having the ability to create wonderful visual schedules, memory books, and social stories while keeping a sense of humor and creativity is *Strip Designer*'s specialty. Thanks to *Strip Designer*, visual supports do not have to be boring. Begin by selecting a template. Add resize, rotate photos within the template cells, add text balloons, captions, and/or cartoon exclamations. *Strip Designer* gives users the ability to be clever, be innovative, and be original. After your masterpiece is complete, share it with friends and family via email or social networking.

iREWARD

by Grembe Inc.

www.grembe.com

$4.99

FROM THE DEVELOPER

How does *iReward* work? Choose the behavior you are trying to reinforce, choose your reward, and then choose the number of times the behavior needs to be completed before the reward is earned.

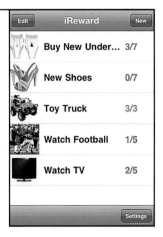

CUSTOMER REVIEW

Who does not want to earn the Golden Ticket? *iReward* puts the effectiveness of a visual reinforcement chart in an easy-to-use app. Whether you choose an image from your camera roll or Google Image Search, *iReward* is a snap to customize to reflect individual likes and motivators. Lock out unintentional taps in Lockable settings using a password. *iReward* is a highly recommended visual reinforcement system for students with autism, developmental delays, yourself, or anyone who could use a little motivation to achieve their goals. Verbal praise and/or a cute cat video is given after completing a set number of stars.

STORIES2LEARN®

by MDR

www.*look2learn*.com

$13.99

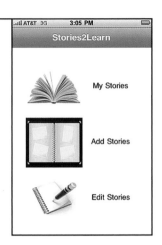

FROM THE DEVELOPER

Stories2Learn (S2L) offers parents and educators the ability to create personalized stories using photos, text, and audio messages. These stories can be used to build literacy, for leisure, as well as developing social skills. In addition, *S2L* comes preloaded with a story illustrating the skills necessary to play a game with a friend.

CUSTOMER REVIEW

This is a good app for creating social stories, memory stories, concepts, and story boards. It comes with one preloaded story. *Stories2Learn* can be used for both verbal and non-verbal individuals. Sound and picture customization is easy. This app is really easy to use with an iPhone because of the built-in camera. If using an iPod touch or iPad, it takes a few more steps to transfer the pictures to the device. *Stories2Learn* has a very helpful tutorial on their website to help you get started.

FIRST THEN VISUAL SCHEDULE

by Good Karma Applications

http://goodkarmaapplications.com

$9.99

FROM THE DEVELOPER

The *First Then Visual Schedule* application is designed for caregivers to provide positive behavior support for those with communication needs. This application provides an affordable and convenient audio-visual prompting tool for use on the iPhone or iPod touch. The portability of the iPhone and iPod touch and ease of use of the application make it perfect for use at school, home, or in the community.

CUSTOMER REVIEW

First Then Visual Schedule is one of the best apps for individuals who need visual input to increase independence, promote understanding of upcoming events, and decrease anxiety during transitions. The user is able to customize both images and audio to fit their unique needs. I use *First Then Visual Schedule* for field trips, high anxiety transitions, and to support hygiene goals. Schedules can also be created on the iPhone (built-in camera) in real time and reviewed later to reinforce learning, memory, and carry-over. *First Then Visual Schedule* offers three formats that can be changed at the touch of a finger.

FIRST THEN VISUAL SCHEDULE (continued)

- Full Screen: One image appears on the screen and the user swipes their finger to access the next image.

- Split Screen: This format shows two images side-by-side or top to bottom. This is the visual used most often in a picture schedule; for example, "First math, then computer."

- List Screen: This screen allows four images to be placed on a schedule.

Recommended for all individuals who can benefit from visual support at home, school, or in the community.

STORYKIT

by ICDL Foundation

http://en.childrenslibrary.org

FREE

FROM THE DEVELOPER

Create an electronic storybook. Make use of the little gaps in life—on the sofa after dinner, in the back seat of the car, or on a train—to do something creative together.

CUSTOMER REVIEW

Instantly create eBooks with *StoryKit*. You can create a story: write some text, illustrate with a picture or drawing, and/or record your own words and sounds. *StoryKit* includes four children's books that can also be modified by the user. If you do not like the ending to "The Three Little Pigs," just change it. After you have created your own story or modified an existing one, share it with friends and family via email. *StoryKit* is also an awesome tool for creating memory books, social stories, and visual schedules. Easy to use and the price is right—it's free.

OMNIGRAFFLE

by The Omni Group

www.omnigroup.com/products/omnigraffle-iPad

$49.99 (30-day money back guarantee)

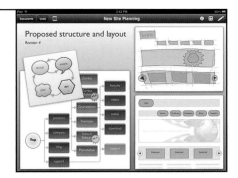

FROM THE DEVELOPER

Need to create a quick diagram, process chart, page layout, website wireframe, or graphic design? With *OmniGraffle*, your iPad Touch screen is your canvas (or graph paper, or whiteboard).

CUSTOMER REVIEW

This app is at the top end of the price scale, but for good reason. *OmniGraffle* is one of the deepest and most complex apps available for making complex visual supports such as concept maps, graphic organizers, schedules, webs, bubble, and Venn diagrams to help students expand their ideas into written expression. Visual learning techniques and visual supports help students to clarify their thinking and to process, organize, and prioritize information. *OmniGraffle* can be used by the educator to create visual supports or by students to help organize thoughts for projects and class work. Once visual supports are designed, the user can share via email, or email as a scalable PDF and save as a graphic in your photo library.

iTHOUGHTSHD (MINDMAPPING)

by CMS

www.iPadmindmap.com/iPadMindmap

$9.99

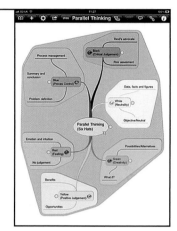

FROM THE DEVELOPER

Mindmapping enables you to visually organize your thoughts, ideas, and information.

CUSTOMER REVIEW

Create large maps with many topics or simple lists with *iThoughtsHD*. Customize, colorize, size, cut, paste, and share visual supports for projects and thought organization. *iThoughtsHD* is great for junior high, high school, or college students who can visually organize information to complete classroom assignments.

GOAL TRACKER

by Twiddly Bits Software LLC

www.twiddlybitssoftware.com

$2.99

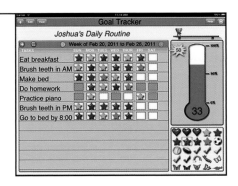

FROM THE DEVELOPER

Goal Tracker helps you focus on your daily tasks. It can be used to track good behavior, a set of chores, a daily routine, or other personal daily goals. You can also set goals for improving your healthy eating habits, taking medicine daily, drinking enough water, or whatever you choose.

CUSTOMER REVIEW

Goal Tracker is useful for parents, educators, and therapists to visually track progress. If you or your child needs structure, consistent routines, and tangible, visible feedback on his or her progress toward goals, then *Goal Tracker* is for you. Users can personalize a challenge according to ability, set a reward, and place stickers as each task is completed.

 There is no lockout function. Stars can be unintentionally added by the user.

VISULES

by Dean Huff

http://sites.google.com/site/deanashuff/Visules

$4.99

FROM THE DEVELOPER

As a father of a child with autism spectrum disorder, I have learned that communicating visually with my son is often the most effective way. As a professional application developer and avid iPhone user, I knew we needed to have "an app for that." The result is *Visules*, which communicates checklists and individual cues using text, images, and colors.

CUSTOMER REVIEW

Visules can easily create Flows (visual schedules, social stories, and story boards) by vertically stringing actions (graphics or pictures), and is easy to customize.

 There is no audio at this time. As steps are completed, they can be checked off. This is a good app for beginning users. The occupational therapists I work with recommend this app for the activities of daily living.

Chapter 16: Visual Timers

Visual timers are used to support time-prediction challenges and transition difficulties at all ages and ability levels. One can see the time elapse and judge time without having to know how to tell the time. I have chosen two very different yet highly effective timers to include in this chapter. There are a myriad of others to choose from. Check them out and choose the most fitting for your needs.

TIME TIMER

by Time Timer LLC

www.timetimer.com

$4.99

FROM THE DEVELOPER

Make every moment count, in education, in business, in life … with the new *Time Timer* application. *Time Timer* delivers an innovative and practical way to address the universal question of, "How much longer?" With the *Time Timer*'s patented "visual-disc" technology, you don't just tell time. You see the passage of time. Its clear-cut, visual cue is its strength. For children and adults.

CUSTOMER REVIEW

Time Timer is the industry standard. This timer is used almost exclusively in schools and clinics. We all know it and love it. The time durations are easily changed; however, it would be nice if I could set the *Time Timer* with my finger instead of having to go into the settings mode. *Time Timer* offers a variety of tones/alarms and three modes to choose from.

iHOURGLASS

by Headlight Software, Inc.

www.ftponthego.com/ihourglass.php

$1.99

FROM THE DEVELOPER

Sand and glass hourglasses are so 14th century! Bring your games into the 21st century and be the envy of everyone at your next game night with *iHourglass*. It all animates beautifully. The sand piles up, and turning it on the side to pause makes all the sand pour to the side. *iHourglass* instantly resets when you flip it upside down, so there's no more waiting for sand to move in order to start the next round in a game!

CUSTOMER REVIEW

Don't tell *Time Timer*, but my students like this timer better. *iHourglass* was originally designed for board games. My students and I like to watch the sand fall through the hourglass. It even has a countdown warning when time is almost up (last five seconds). There are seven cool designs to choose from. Try the free version, then decide if *iHourglass* fits your needs.

Chapter 17:
Sound Masking

Some individuals with disabilities, autism in particular, have a high level of sensitivity to noise. Relatively quiet noises may cause an individual to cover his or her ears, run away, or contribute to a meltdown. Sound Masking works on the principle that disturbing noises can be reduced by constant noise in the background. Relaxing tapes, soothing sounds, or white noise can help with noisy settings and difficult transitions. Parents and caregivers have reported good success with noise-masking apps when traveling or transitioning into loud environments.

SOUNDCURTAIN

by FutureAcoustic

www.futureacoustic.com

$3.99

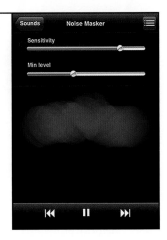

FROM THE DEVELOPER

SoundCurtain is a unique application that masks distracting noise by automatically adapting its volume, pitch, and tone in response to the noise around you. It comes with seven generative tracks featuring intelligent, self-adjusting white noise and harmonic sounds that listen and react to your environment.

CUSTOMER REVIEW

Does your child cover his or her ears, run away, cry, or have meltdowns in noisy environments? If so, try *SoundCurtain* to make noisy transitions and rowdy environments tolerable. *SoundCurtain* adjusts to the noise in your environment by monitoring through your headset microphone and performing real-time analysis of the background noise. Individuals who are sound sensitive usually need to wear noise reduction headphones. These headphones usually do the trick, but they are large, expensive, and obvious. *SoundCurtain* helps the user tolerate noisy environments without looking different.

AMBIANCE

by Urban Apps

http://ambiance.urbanapps.com

$2.99

FROM THE DEVELOPER

Ambiance is an "environment enhancer" designed to help you create the perfect ambient atmosphere to focus, relax, or reminisce.

CUSTOMER REVIEW

With a huge collection of over 100 sounds, *Ambiance* can help drown out the clamor around you. Sound sensitive individuals may find it easier to transition into loud environments with the aid of *Ambiance*. Parents have had success using sound-masking apps to help their children cope with environmental noise without using headphones or earplugs.

 Ambiance does not have any included sample sounds. You can download as many free sounds from the server as you want—if you have an Internet connection. If you do not have access to a Wifi connection, you will not be able to get new sounds into *Ambiance*.

Part VI

Apps for Occupational Therapy

When did computer games and learning become synonymous? Thanks to technology we are able to use a multitude of devices to enhance the learning experience. Most recently, the iPad has become a popular, and my favorite, tool to use during occupational therapy sessions with school-aged children. First, I will describe the role of a school-based occupational therapist and some of the areas we address within this setting. Secondly, I'll explain how we can incorporate the use of an iPad into our children's activities of daily living.

A school-based occupational therapist is a part of a multidisciplinary educational team. Our primary role is to facilitate a person's ability to participate in the activities of daily life or their "occupations." Many parents have said, "What is my child's occupation?" Well, I always explain that school, learning, and play is their full-time job for the next 13 years. Their job description requires them to maintain their attention span, listen, read, write, interact with peers, and most importantly, play!

When there is a child who experiences challenges in one or more of the areas above, sometimes the child has to receive some job-coaching in order to maximize his or her school experience. This is where an occupational therapist comes into play, literally. Once the child is assessed and qualified for services, the occupational therapist will determine which areas the child needs assistance in.

Typically, in a school-based setting, the areas we primarily assess are fine motor skills and sensory processing abilities. There are many components to fine motor skills, but the two that are most used in early education are writing and typing. In order to learn writing and typing, a child must be able to filter out distractions to maintain their attention span, which may become compromised within a classroom setting. Examples of common distractions include fire drills, loud talking, and unexpected touching from peers. Furthermore, a child must be able to maintain effective posturing, participate in tactile activities, and engage in a variety of movements during the school "work" day. This is when we need the ability to adapt our senses to what is happening in our environment.

So how does the iPad come into play, literally? Used with many other treatment techniques, the iPad can be used to assist with a child's fine motor and sensory processing deficits. There are endless apps that are used to promote handwriting as well as the underlying skills that support handwriting. These games allow a child to cross midline, bilaterally coordinate use of hands, increase body awareness, increase spatial awareness, require motor planning, etc. A few of the apps that are used in occupational therapy sessions include *Doodle Buddy*, *IWriteWords*, *MeMoves*, *Proloquo2Go*, *Tilt Maze*, *MazeFinger*, *Dressing Teddy*, and the list goes on. When using the iPad as an iTherapy tool please make sure to consult with a speech or occupational therapist to ensure maximum benefit.

—by Gina Banks OTR/L

Chapter 18: Handwriting

Individuals with disabilities face an extra hurdle; they often lack the fine motor coordination required for handwriting, which will likely lead to problems with self esteem and academic performance. Occupational therapists have tried many different "programs" to encourage students to write better. The "programs" are good; however, students sometimes lack motivation. Then came the iPad. Students will literally wait in line for a chance to practice writing. Some students will work and earn the iPad so that they can practice their writing. Students can use their finger or a stylus, whichever fits their individual needs and abilities. There is an abundance of handwriting apps on the market. Choose one, or more than one, to meet your goals. I guarantee no tears.

Success Story: Bonnie

I have worked with Bonnie for many years. She is a nine-year-old student with autism who frequently has challenging behaviors due to frustration. She can read and type at about the first grade level. Her speech consists of unintelligible movie and TV lines. She uses, but does not carry, a traditional voice-output device to communicate wants (computer, swing, outside, and Jump Start). Initially she did not write.

I introduced Bonnie to the iPad and she instantly chose *ABC Tracer*. She sat in a beanbag and completed each letter, upper and lower case. She is a perfectionist, so every letter had to be perfect. Bonnie now writes (pencil and paper) in phrases, and has another modality to communicate. Bonnie will also frequently use *Speak it!*, *ABA Flashcards*, *Lunch Box*, *Feed Me*, *Listen to Music*, *Read a Book* and flip through the apps with ease. Bonnie knows her limits with the iPad and will give it back when finished, about 30-40 minutes. Bonnie's teacher is using the iPad to introduce math concepts. Bonnie will carry the iPad Touch and iPad to any destination with no protests. Fantastic!

Ray Hart, an 11-year-old West Prairie South Elementary student, works on an iPad. An education app, abcPocket-Phonics, has helped Ray improve his writing.

In the News

Students with Autism Find Help with iPad

—by Lainie Steelman

On a recent Monday morning at West Prairie South Elementary in Colchester, Illinois, Ray Hart, 11, used a stylus to trace a small "t" on an iPad screen. After he successfully traced the letter, the tablet computer made a cheering sound. Ray looked up at his teacher, Lori Thompson, and smiled. Working on the iPad has helped Hart dramatically improve his handwriting and boost his confidence.

"The first time I showed this to one little guy—and he is verbal—he was able to start writing letters, and that's carried over into his paper work," Thompson said.

Most of the students in Thompson's special needs classroom have autism, a developmental disorder that makes communication and social interaction difficult.

"We're always looking for new ways to help our students come up with ways to communicate and be motivated," Thompson said. "We have another (nonverbal) student who uses an augmentative communication device that's very heavy and bulky and hard to carry around, so we were looking for an alternative."

Thompson's two iPads were received after West Prairie Superintendent Jonathan Heerboth suggested the idea.

"There was an article in the San Francisco Chronicle that talked about iPads as a useful communication tool for children on the autism spectrum who could not otherwise communicate," Heerboth said. "I knew that Mrs. Thompson had experimented with a similar idea on her iPod touch."

After Thompson researched the idea, an Apple sales representative met with Heerboth, Thompson, and one of her students after the new school year started in August. Soon, Thompson was able to buy two iPads—at a considerably lower cost than other augmentative communication devices.

"The other devices are from $3,000 to $5,000 dollars apiece," Thompson said. "iPads cost, depending on how much memory you get, $500 and up."

Thompson's nonverbal student uses the iPad with a text-to-speech application called *Proloquo2Go*. Using this application, Thompson's nonverbal student can easily participate in class and answer questions by touching the appropriate icon on the iPad, which then voices a response.

"If it's their day to be calendar helper, they can tell us," Thompson said. "They can pick the day of the week, they can tell me what the weather is (and) they can participate in the Pledge of Allegiance all by touch, and that's very exciting for them."

Another application on Hart's iPad, called abc *PocketPhonics*, not only teaches him how to write a letter, but it teaches him the sound. *Stories2Learn* teaches social cues, something kids with autism find difficult to pick up on. With this application, Thompson can create a simple story using a combination of photos and her own text that shows a specific skill, such as eye contact. If she chooses, Thompson can also narrate the stories with her own voice. Thompson can create her own pages for the iPad. If she's doing a lesson on spiders, for example, she can create a page about spiders in about 15 minutes.

"The apps are easy to download from iTunes and some other places as well," Thompson said. "It's a lot easier than some of the DynaVox (communication) systems I'm used to programming."

Many of these applications can also be downloaded onto an iPhone or iPod touch, and most are inexpensive. *abc PocketPhonics* costs just $1.99 on iTunes, for example, and *Stories2Learn* is available for $13.99. *Proloquo2Go*, a more specialized application, costs $189.99.

The iPads stay in the classroom and do not go home with the students. They are recharged at the end of the day and, if needed, Thompson updates them with new material.

Kathy Olesen-Tracey, an educator with the Center for Application of Information Technology at Western Illinois University, said current research is showing that the use of technologies such as the iPad, and even smart phones like the iPhone, improves student test scores. She cited one recent study that showed high school students who used math applications with smart phones received higher standardized test scores in math.

Tracey says "assistive technology," like the iPad, doesn't replace teaching in classrooms, it reinforces it.

"You're creating an entire network they can tap into," she said.

The iPads in Thompson's classroom have been so successful that she wants all of her students to have access to the technology.

"We're working on trying to write a grant to get a couple more," Thompson said.

ABC POCKETPHONICS: LETTER SOUNDS & WRITING + FIRST WORDS

by Apps in My Pocket Ltd.

www.appsinmypocket.com

$1.99

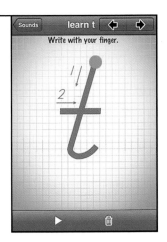

FROM THE DEVELOPER

Only *abc PocketPhonics* follows the "synthetic phonics" teaching method—the keystone of the "Reading First" part of the "No Child Left Behind" Act. *abc PocketPhonics* was designed and reviewed by U.S. and U.K. teachers who use phonics to teach children to read. It is primarily aimed at preschool kids.

CUSTOMER REVIEW

I have heard folks say that their child learned to read and write using *abc PocketPhonics*. I agree; *PocketPhonics* is a very good, phonics-based, beginning reader app. This app teaches sounds, sound blending and letter formation. The letter formation portion is a bit strict. You will have to try again if you go too far off the line. Students can use a stylus to practice letter formation and writing skills utilizing a tripod grasp. The audio is clean and sound effects are low key. If you are not sure if your student/child will enjoy this app try the free version first. *PocketPhonics* also offers a free guide to teaching children to read.

iWRITEWORDS (HANDWRITING GAME)

by gdiplus

http://gdiplus.ptgdi.com/iWriteWords.html

$2.99

FROM THE DEVELOPER

iWriteWords teaches your child handwriting while playing a fun and entertaining game. Help Mr. Crab collect the numbers in sequence by dragging him with your finger and drawing the letter at the same time. Once all the letters in the word are drawn properly, a cute drawing appears. Tilt your iPhone or iPod touch and watch the letters slide into the rotating hole and advance to the next level.

CUSTOMER REVIEW

iWriteWords is motivating for individuals who are learning writing, alphabet, and beginning reading skills. *iWriteWords* offers plenty of entertaining practice with a game-type impression. The audio can be unclear with an echo quality; most younger students like the sounds, but most adults will turn it down. The target word, letter, or number is shown in the upper left-hand corner. The user traces the target following a cute crab with their finger in a numeric sequence. When the tracing is complete, the target falls from the top corner and the user guides it to the right bottom corner to advance to the next level. Settings are in the main menu to avoid unintentional setting changes. Features the user can choose from consist of numbers, words, letters, upper case and lower case. *iWriteWords* is entertaining, educational, and supports fine motor skills. Try the free version to see if this app is right for you.

LETTER LAB

by Critical Matter, Inc.

www.criticalmatter.com

$2.99

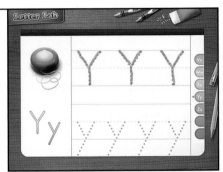

FROM THE DEVELOPER

Letter Lab is the ideal application for children learning to write and recognize their ABC's. You can intuitively trace both uppercase and lowercase letters with the touch of a finger, as well as hear and see English alphabet letters and real world objects that relate to them.

CUSTOMER REVIEW

Letter Lab is a good tool for practicing writing skills with just your finger or a stylus. No bells or whistles, just practice. *Letter Lab* is an alternative to the paper and pencil. The user can change crayon color, erase, change letters, and hear the name of the object and letter with a touch of the finger.

 The erase function will erase all work on the page. Some students want to erase only the last letter they traced due to a mistake. Last thing, a model of the correct pen stroke would make occupational therapists very happy.

Chapter 19:
Bilateral Coordination

Bilateral coordination is the use of both sides of the body together to perform a task efficiently and is necessary for writing, cutting, typing, and most academic and vocational activities. Bilateral coordination can be facilitated by any activity that utilizes both the right and left arms working together to complete a task. Nobody said this couldn't be fun. Note: *Doodle Jump, Scoops, Tilt Maze, Crash Bandicoot* and most "games" capture data by keeping score and building on acquired skills and levels. Remember, terms like high score, levels, or total scoops are not norms-based and will need to be converted into percentages and prompt levels.

MEMOVES

by Thinking Moves

www.thinkingmoves.com

$2.99

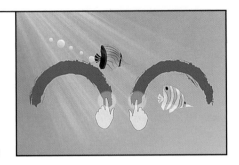

Perform finger puzzles correctly to the beat of the music and watch as the screen comes alive. Based on the award-winning *MeMoves* DVD, the *MeMoves* app can provide instant calm and focus anywhere. For ages three through 103.

CUSTOMER REVIEW

Simple, unique, and tranquil. Help your students with sensory integration needs, ASD, depression, and anxiety to relax, calm down, and focus attention. *MeMoves* also allows teachers, therapists, and parents to refocus and re-energize. Thirty different finger puzzles are combined with soothing music and 2D/3D graphics to accomplish a "centered" state of being. *MeMoves* is also wonderful for increasing short attention spans and preparing busy brains to begin challenging tasks. *MeMoves* is one of the sharpest tools in the tool-box for bilateral coordination and pre-writing activities.

ABC MAZE

by gdiplus

http://gdiplus.ptgdi.com/ABC_Maze.html

$1.99

FROM THE DEVELOPER

Control Birdie by tilting your iPhone or iPod touch and help him catch all the runaway letters.

CUSTOMER REVIEW

ABC Maze puts a great spin on spelling, letter recognition, labeling, and bilateral coordination. The user guides an adorable round birdie to the letters by tilting the iDevice back and forth, up and down. After the birdie has found all the letters, the word is spelled out, and a picture of the word appears. The sound effects are futuristic; however, the audio voiceover is breathy and the volume varies. I know how to read, spell, and label, yet I find myself playing this game in my spare time. Recommended for students learning their ABCs, beginning readers, and individuals with motor challenges. *ABC Maze* offers a free trial version of this game. Try it, you'll like it!

DOODLE JUMP—BE WARNED: INSANELY ADDICTIVE!

by Lima Sky

www.limasky.com

$0.99

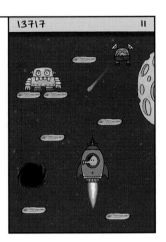

FROM THE DEVELOPER

In *Doodle Jump*™, you guide Doodle the Doodler™—using some of the most subtle and accurate tilt controls in existence—on a springy journey up, up, up a sheet of graph paper, picking up jet packs, avoiding black holes, and blasting baddies with nose balls along the way.

CUSTOMER REVIEW

Doodle Jump is one of the most popular apps in America. Your students can practice bilateral coordination while guiding their Doodle in an upward journey into the unknown. *Doodle Jump* is easy to play; simply tilt your device left or right, and tap the screen to shoot. When your student gets good at jumping, add distracters such as walking, talking, using only one hand, or playing at different angles.

 I've heard *Doodle Jump* is addicting.

SCOOPS—ICE CREAM FUN FOR EVERYONE

by NimbleBit

www.nimblebit.com

FREE

FROM THE DEVELOPER

Over a million people are screaming for ice cream! Stack your ice cream cone high into the sky by tilting the phone left and right, catching as many scoops as you can while avoiding the vegetables (veggies ARE great apart from ice cream!). The higher you go, the faster they fall, and the more wobbly your tower! Stack similar colors together for extra points.

CUSTOMER REVIEW

Who knew? An app that is challenging and entertaining could be beneficial. *Scoops–Ice Cream Fun for Everyone* not only targets grins, but bilateral coordination, muscle grading, turn-taking, and friendly competition. Compare your scores with the world. Occupational therapists seem to get all the cool game apps.

 Updates are not free. New themes are 99 cents.

TILT MAZE

by Exact Magic Software, LLC

www.exactmagic.com/products/tilt-maze

$0.99

FROM THE DEVELOPER

Tilt Maze is a fast and easy-to-play maze game. Just tilt your iPhone or iPod touch to move your marble through the labyrinth to the exit

CUSTOMER REVIEW

Tilt Maze has 20 colorful mazes that will challenge your bilateral coordination, balance, muscle grading, and visual perception. When a student gets good at moving the marble through the labyrinth, try playing while walking, standing on one leg, with one eye closed, or with one hand.

CRASH BANDICOOT NITRO KART 3D

by Activision Publishing, Inc.

www.activision.com

$2.99

FROM THE DEVELOPER

The richest 3D kart racing experience! Speed your way through 12 thrilling tracks and multiple environments! Race and battle against zany opponents and turn them to dust with eight devastating weapons. Tilt and twist your iPhone for truly "Nitro" driving sensations.

CUSTOMER REVIEW

Crash Bandicoot Nitro Kart 3D is highly motivating and good for bilateral coordination and wrist strength. As students get good at driving *Crash Bandicoot*, the occupational therapist may have them walk down the hall and play the game to improve multitasking. Options on *Nitro Kart* include sound, vibration, language, accelerometer, and visual effects. Recommended for students who like a challenge. I suggest that students take the tutorial prior to starting a game.

 This app is stimulating for both sight and sound.

Chapter 20:
Motor Planning

Motor planning is the ability of the brain to organize and carry out a sequence of unfamiliar actions. Motor planning with iTherapy targets eye-hand coordination, grading, timing, finger isolation, and sequencing of the upper extremities (hands and arms). It has been my and my colleagues' experience that individuals are so highly motivated to use iDevices that they will not give up or get frustrated on failed attempts or require additional reinforcement to participate in motor planning activities. Every activity that an individual does with an iDevice can be considered motor planning. Be that as it may, here are some apps that have concentrated motor planning power.

SLIDE 2 UNLOCK

by RJ Cooper & Associates, Inc.

www.rjcooper.com

$0.99

FROM THE DEVELOPER

Slide 2 Unlock is a great iPad teaching aid for people who need help practicing and/or understanding how to unlock their iPad.

CUSTOMER REVIEW

Unlocking your iPad is an essential step in accessing all the "magical" qualities of your device. *Slide 2 Unlock* breaks the process of unlocking your device into five steps (games). Each step takes the user closer to the goal. *Slide 2 Unlock* can be used in portrait and landscape. The two final steps/games allow the user to choose the background currently on the lock screen to support generalization. I find that I can usually skip the first two steps; however, I am glad they are there if needed. Recommended for individuals who need support mastering the swipe motion for unlocking and navigating through apps on their devices.

UZU

by Colordodge Labs

http://uzumotion.com

$1.99

Technically speaking, *Uzu* is a kinetic multitouch particle visualizer. Really, it's a sort-of math-physics-art-toy for anyone who ever loved spirographs, fireworks, planetariums, lava lamps, lightsabers, pen lasers, tesla coils, Christmas lights, or graphing calculators.

There are ten Modes of Control:

- 1 Touch: emanate and radiate
- 2 Touch: pinch attraction and boundary bounce
- 3 Touch: tri-point vortex
- 4 Touch: quad-point inverted vortex
- 5 Touch: 3D freeze and translate
- 6 Touch: 3D oscillating mass
- 7 Touch: 3D tri-arm spiral
- 8 Touch: 3D warp and inverted translate
- 9 Touch: 9 springy space ribbons
- 10 Touch: change color and particle size

CUSTOMER REVIEW

Uzu is visually stunning! *Uzu* is a fabulous occupational therapy tool for sensory and motor control (see modes of control below). My students will work through several stacks of flashcards just to have a few minutes with *Uzu*. *Uzu* is highly recommended for everyone.

KNOTS

by Josh Snyder

http://twitter.com/treelinelabs

FREE

FROM THE DEVELOPER

Tie your fingers in knots with this classic iPhone game. When a spot appears, touch and hold until it disappears … and keep extra fingers at the ready! Or get your fingers intertwined in two-player mode.

CUSTOMER REVIEW

Knots is Twister for your fingers. Play alone or with a friend. Playing this game will increase finger isolation, eye-hand coordination, social interaction, and friendly competition. Simply place a finger on a dot when it appears and remove it when the dot disappears (illustrated by rings around the dot).

 The user will need a few trials before understanding the game rules. See the "How to Play" section embedded in the app. *Knots* has been used successfully by students with Asperger's syndrome to encourage social interaction and strengthen finger dexterity.

DOODLE BUDDY—PAINT, DRAW, SCRIBBLE, SKETCH

by Pinger, Inc.

www.pinger.com/content/apps.html

FREE

FROM THE DEVELOPER

Doodle Buddy is the most fun you can have with your finger!
Finger paint with your favorite color and drop in playful stamps.
Connect with a friend to draw together over the Internet.

CUSTOMER REVIEW

Doodle Buddy is the app that broke the ice with many of my students. Once they discovered that they could magically draw and stamp with their finger, they were hooked on the devices. Occupational therapists use *Doodle Buddy* for such things as eye-hand coordination, motor control, and finger isolation. I have never had to give any instructions with this app. Students at all levels seem to intrinsically know how to change colors, find stamps, and adjust the line size. In addition, I use *Doodle Buddy* in place of a white board. No dry erase marker or eraser needed, simply shake to erase and begin again. Easy, motivating, therapeutic, and free!

FISH FINGERS! 3D INTERACTIVE AQUARIUM

by www.UselessiPhoneStuff.com

www.uselessiPhonestuff.com

$0.99

FROM THE DEVELOPER

Interact with your fish! Touch the screen and watch the fish follow your finger. Double tap the screen to feed them; they'll slowly grow if you do! Use any image you like as the background to your aquarium! Simply select any image from your photo library and it'll look like your iPhone is full of water, and full of 3D fish!

CUSTOMER REVIEW

Fish Fingers! lets you practice motor control and relax at the same time. The very clever occupational therapist puts shapes and letters in the background and has the students move the fish along the shapes/letters to practice formation.

 The fish do not move quickly. Therefore, *Fish Fingers* is a lesson in controlled, purposeful movement and patience.

WOOLY WILLY

by Paze

http://pazeinteractive.com/iphoneapps/woolywilly

$0.99

FROM THE DEVELOPER

Unleash your creativity on the classic images of Wooly Willy
and Hairdo Harriet or give your friend a makeover by choosing
from your own image library!

CUSTOMER REVIEW

Wooly Willy gives adults a nostalgic good feeling just seeing his face. Occupational therapists have utilized *Wooly Willy* for eye-hand coordination, motor control, finger isolation,
and proprioceptive awareness (the sense of how your own limbs are oriented in space).
Wooly Willy has helped out with creativity, body-part labeling, and provides a reinforcing
leisure time activity. Thanks, *Wooly Willy*! To add motivation, use an image of an individual or known person in place of Wooly Willy.

ANACONDA

by Silver Mana Software

http://silvermanasoft.appspot.com

$0.99

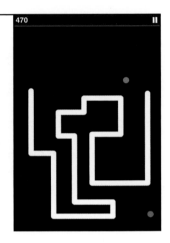

FROM THE DEVELOPER

Try to stay alive while your snake gets both longer and faster. How long can you survive? Control the snake by tapping the screen in the direction you want to go. Red apples are persistent, worth 10 points, and make the snake grow. Yellow apples are persistent, worth 15 points, and make the snake switch directions. Green apples are timed, worth 20 points, and make the snake move faster.

CUSTOMER REVIEW

Anaconda begins simply and progressively gets more difficult as you play. You can choose a background; my favorite is "reverse polarity." Individuals with visual sensory integration challenges may like the "reverse polarity" mode best. Students who play this game are also focusing on eye-hand coordination, visual perceptual abilities, motor planning, and coordination. What a "pain-free" way to achieve occupational therapy goals! *Anaconda* can also be used for a reinforcer—it is highly motivating to play.

ACTIONPOTATO

by Sunflats

www.sunflat.net/iphone/app/actionpotato/?lang=en

FREE

FROM THE DEVELOPER

Catch fresh potatoes to make potato stew! Touch pots to jump and catch potatoes thrown from the right side of the screen. If you catch a rotten potato, you lose the pot! But if you catch a heart, the pot comes back.

CUSTOMER REVIEW

ActionPotato is simple and fun with appealing, clear graphics. Students who play this game have no idea they are targeting eye-hand coordination, motor control, coordination, and visual perceptual skills. Students rarely get frustrated because the potatoes are really easy to catch. Recommended for younger individuals and/or individuals who have motor planning challenges. It's free!

LIGHTSABER UNLEASHED

by TheMacBox

http://themacbox.co.uk/phonesaber

FREE

FROM THE DEVELOPER

Ever wished you could swing your iPhone around like a light-saber? Well now you can, with *Lightsaber Unleashed*! As you swing your phone, a range of Lightsaber™ sound effects will be emitted from your phone's speaker (or connected audio output). Not only that, but you can also draw and withdraw your light saber. You can also choose your *Force Unleashed* character of choice, as well as playing some dueling music to get you in the mood! Last but not least, you can enter a full screen "lightsaber mode," to enhance your light saber experience!

CUSTOMER REVIEW

Some people call this app "cheesy." My friend the occupational therapist calls this app fantastic. She has her students increasing range of motion, crossing midline, and strengthening both fine and gross motor skills.

 Lightsaber Unleashed does not work well on the iPad.

GUITAR HERO

by Activision Publishing, Inc.

http://hub.guitarhero.com/games/ghiPhone

$2.99

FROM THE DEVELOPER

You'll find a robust avatar customization mode that allows you to personalize your in-game rock star and an innovative new play style that challenges you to tap, strum, whammy, and slide your way to the top of the Rock Ranks. *Guitar Hero* for the iPhone and iPod touch is the most authentic guitar and bass experience on the go!

CUSTOMER REVIEW

If you are familiar with the gamer version, then you know this app. It comes with six not very popular songs; however, you can purchase song packs. *Guitar Hero* is used to strengthen eye-hand coordination, motor control, and focus. *Guitar Hero* can be played with the dominant or non-dominant hand, or both hands. I have used this app as a reinforcer. Perhaps the best use of this app I have witnessed, was when a teen with Asperger's syndrome (who usually ate lunch alone) had a crowd of peers gathered around him discussing scores, songs, and gaming systems.

 The characters in *Guitar Hero* are "mature." Check out the screen shots to decide if they are fitting for your child or student.

POCKETGUITAR

by Shinya Kasatani

http://podmap.net/pocketguitar

$0.99

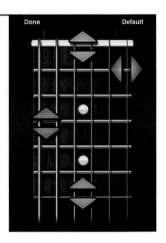

FROM THE DEVELOPER

You can choose the sound from six instruments: acoustic-electric guitar, electric guitar, classical guitar, muted guitar, electric bass, and ukulele. You can also choose effects from distortion, chorus, delay, and edit parameters.

CUSTOMER REVIEW

PocketGuitar has a great sound. I wish this app had a coaching feature so that I could play a simple song. Individuals can strum, pluck, and develop bilateral coordination, motor control, and creativity. Who knows, *PocketGuitar* may inspire individuals to pick up a real guitar.

SPEAK BOT

by Core Engine Apps

www.coreengineapps.com

$0.99

FROM THE DEVELOPER

Speak Bot speaks aloud whatever you type. Make the voice high or low pitch, fast or slow, expressive or monotonous.

CUSTOMER REVIEW

This is how an occupational therapist encourages a student to spend hours practicing keyboarding, spelling, finger isolation, motor skills, and eye-hand coordination. *Speak Bot* offers a variety of voice effects and saving options to play back later. The user can even email messages, jokes, and comments to friends and family via .wav files.

MAZEFINGER PLUS

by ngmoco, Inc

http://*mazefinger*.ngmoco.com

FREE

FROM THE DEVELOPER

Obliterate 1,000 lightning-fast mazes as you unleash the awesome power of your finger! Penetrate a seemingly endless collection of challenging mazes and race to the exit before your energy runs out!

CUSTOMER REVIEW

MazeFinger can be utilized in numerous fashions; however, it is most cherished by occupational therapists for finger isolation, eye-hand coordination, and visual-perceptual skills. *MazeFinger* is visually stimulating and highly motivating to play.

 An account is required to play the game. Also, the robotic voice is difficult to understand and you are labeled "weak" if you take too long.

Chapter 21: Activities of Daily Living (ADLs)

Learning how to perform activities of daily living like cooking, feeding, toileting, and self-care are a crucial part of an individual's education, self-worth, and how the world views him or her. ADLs are an important focus of intervention, especially those surrounding hygiene and feeding. Temple Grandin wrote of an employer who told her that her arm pits stank and gave her a can of Arid deodorant. Even brilliance may not overcome body odor, unwashed hair, or food-stained clothing. The Conover Company has developed the Functional Life Skills series of 19 apps that cover everything from dressing to grooming, and hygiene. I found a few more; so take a look!

MORE PIZZA!

by Maverick Software

www.mavericksw.com

$0.99

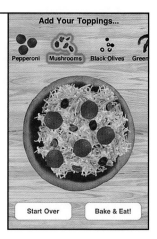

FROM THE DEVELOPER

Turn your iPod touch or iPhone into a pizzeria! Choose your crust, pour on the sauce, add loads of cheese, and all the toppings you want. Then bake it right there in your virtual oven, where it will come out piping hot and ready to slice.

CUSTOMER REVIEW

More Pizza! is an occupational therapist's dream. Motor control, eye-hand coordination, muscle grading, and Activities of Daily Living (ADLs) are all rolled up into one app. This highly motivational app takes the user from choosing the plate, crust, and toppings to cooking, cutting, and finally eating. Directions are provided upon the first use. Speech therapists use *More Pizza!* for labeling, following directions, verbal sequencing, and having fun (social skills). I also have used *More Pizza!* successfully in teaching vocational skills. Students can take orders from their peers, write them down, make the pizza according to order, and serve it. Pizza can even be served remotely to family and friends via email. This is a great, highly recommended app for all ability levels.

If you like *More Pizza!* You will also enjoy the following apps from Maverick Software:

More Sundaes!   More Cupcakes!   More Toast!   More Salad!

——————————— Each is $0.99 ———————————

Each of the above apps takes the user from setup to cooking and eating the desired food. Each food choice has virtually limitless toppings and customization choices. The educational benefits are also limitless. The "More" series of apps promotes increased vocabulary, muscle control, following directions, sequencing, Activities of Daily Living, vocational, leisure activities, and generalization. Enjoy!

CAKE DOODLE & COOKIE DOODLE

by Shoe The Goose

www.shoethegoose.com

$0.99 each

Menu

Carrot Cake

☐ 2 cups flour
☐ 2 cups sugar
☐ 2 teaspoons cinnamon
☐ 2 teaspoons baking powder
☐ 1 cup vegetable oil
☐ 4 eggs
☐ 1 cup chopped pecans
☐ 4 cups grated carrots

Drag ingredients into the bowl.

FROM THE DEVELOPER

Need a cake or cookies in a hurry for that special occasion? Love to decorate, but hate the dirty pans, messy counters, and hot kitchen? *Cake Doodle* and *Cookie Doodle* are the answer! Crack the eggs, shake the salt, pour in the liquids, and toss in the dry ingredients. Blend the batter and bake in our super fast oven. No need to wait to cool before icing and decorating it.

CUSTOMER REVIEW

Both *Cake Doodle* and *Cookie Doodle* provide a wealth of educational and recreational opportunities. The Doodle apps promote following directions, motor control, grading, Activities of Daily Living, vocabulary, sequencing, and creativity, just to name a few important skills. The user moves through mixing the batter from a recipe, then baking, and finally decorating, making individual choices all along the way. After you have completed your culinary masterpiece, you can email it to your mom, dad, grandma, or best friend along with a message. Best of all, there is no mess or dirty dishes in the sink. Don't forget to eat them!

Nutrition Facts:
Calories.............................0
Total Fat............................0 g

Cholesterol ....0 mg
Total Carbohydrate.........................0 g
Protein ....0 g

DRESS-UP

by fishdog.net

http://fishdog.net/dress-up

$0.99

FROM THE DEVELOPER

Good, clean fun for preschool boys and girls at a great price. Kids can choose outfits and color combinations and patterns by tapping and dragging clothes and accessories on the screen. Boy and girl dolls are included.

CUSTOMER REVIEW

Dress-up is simple, yet effective in teaching vocabulary and concept development. Nouns, categories, descriptors, and prepositions can be targeted while creating outfits and color combinations for the girl and boy dolls. While dressing and/or undressing your doll, clothing and accessories fall into place easily. Try before you buy with the free version.

HOW DIRTY ARE YOU?

by Trippert Labs

www.trippertlabs.com

FREE

FROM THE DEVELOPER

Are you nauseatingly filthy or are you too clean? Find out where you stand on the hygiene scale! Remember, this app is for entertainment purposes only. Enjoy! ☺

CUSTOMER REVIEW

Personal hygiene is not an easy subject to bring up. The *How Dirty Are You?* app is a light-hearted way to introduce and discuss the sensitive issue of personal hygiene. This app asks the user a series of questions; each question has four choices. At the end of the ten question series the user is rated for dirtiness.

 How Dirty Are You? is meant for entertainment purposes only. We use it as a fun way to introduce Activities of Daily Living.

DRESSING TEDDY

by Portegno Apps

www.portegno-apps.com

$0.99

FROM THE DEVELOPER

You can now dress up this cute Teddy Bear. You can change colors, hats, faces, shirts, and lots of more cute objects.

CUSTOMER REVIEW

This cute teddy bear makes activities of daily living and dressing for the day entertaining. *Dressing Teddy* also provides opportunities for labeling, describing, finger isolation, and motor coordination. And you thought you were just having fun! Recommended for the young and young-at-heart.

COOKING MAMA

by TAITO Corporation

www.taito.co.jp

$6.99

FROM THE DEVELOPER

Cooking Mama includes two fun game modes: "Let's Cook," where players make meals with Mama, and "Cooking Contest," where players can freely practice a variety of recipes and techniques.

CUSTOMER REVIEW

Cooking Mama is being used by occupational therapists for improving motor skills and activities of daily living. *Cooking Mama* is very interactive as the user has to touch (chop), shake (knead/shape), and tilt (spread or melt butter) the device to accomplish a task.

 I have heard that *Cooking Mama* has glitches. I have had no problems yet. Try the free version before committing to the entire app.

FUNCTIONAL SKILLS SYSTEM (42 APPS)

by The Conover Company

www.conovercompany.com/ipod/apps

- Functional Life Skills (19 Apps)
- Functional Literacy Skills (7 Apps)
- Functional Social Skills (6 Apps)
- Functional Work Skills (3 Apps)
- Functional Math Skills (3 Apps)
- Functional Skills Sampler (4 Apps)

All are $0.99 each, but the Sampler is FREE

FROM THE DEVELOPER

For some, going on a shopping trip, using basic literacy skills, understanding what to do when seeing a warning sign, or transitioning from school to work, are very difficult tasks. The *Functional Skills System* software provides easy-to-understand information that allows learners to become more capable of functioning independently in their homes, schools, communities, and workplaces. This system increases a learner's ability to make appropriate choices. Gaining functional literacy, social, life, and work skills allows for freedom and independence. These programs are for anyone trying to become more functionally independent in our society.

 Conover Company will be releasing a Shopping List generator, a Daily Activity List generator and a Communication tool shortly.

FUNCTIONAL SKILLS SYSTEM (continued)

Finally, I can take social skills into the community where they belong and practice in real time and in natural situations. Video modeling has proven to be a fast, effective training method for teaching tasks to individuals with autism and those who require visual supports for success. Students on the spectrum are often unable to absorb information or maintain attention through a one-on-one, or classroom demonstration. *Functional Skills Sampler* provides individuals on the spectrum the visual support they need to practice a skill until it is mastered. And now it is easy to practice at home, school, and with parents and educators to encourage generalization and success.

Part VII

General Education

Tomas Todd is a classroom teacher for young adults with cognitive and behavioral challenges. Thomas uses both the iPhone and iPad extensively and effectively for academic and vocational goals. This is what Thomas has to say regarding this new assistive technology:

As a special education classroom teacher, it is my responsibility to educate my students in a way that addresses their individual needs and differences. Through the years I have had many assistive technology professionals come to my classroom and recommend expensive specialty equipment. The school purchases the equipment, and it is delivered to my classroom. More than likely, I will never see that assistive technology specialist again, and the equipment will not get used for more than a month or two.

Finally, things have changed. I purchased an iPhone several years ago and by mistake left it on my desk while I was preparing for lunchtime. When I returned to my desk, I noticed that a student had taken the iPhone and was quietly engaging in an audio book app. Since that day I have used my iPhone and new iPad daily with my students. Most of the class did not need instructions on how to use the devices. I have successfully met or exceeded reading, writing, math, and vocational goals. Students will complete classroom tasks to have access to the devices; they can navigate successfully from apps to the web and never, ever use the iDevices inappropriately. As John Ruskin said, "Education is the leading of human souls to what is best, and making what is best out of them."

—Thomas Todd, M.A., SpecEd

Chapter 22: Reading

Teaching reading to individuals with disabilities can be challenging and time consuming; however, it is well worth the effort. Every student will learn at an individual pace and programming should be age-appropriate, interactive, and functional. Some students will read before they talk; however, they may not understand what they have read. It has been suggested that students with autism are "hardwired" to read because of their strong visual skills. Therefore, just because students do not verbalize, do not assume that they cannot learn to read.

Success Story: Karl

Karl is a 20-year-old male student with profound visual and sensory challenges. Karl has not been able to tolerate toileting and attempts to encourage independence have been unsuccessful. Using Karl's two favorite stories—"Shrek" from *iStoryTime* and "The Cask of Amontillado" on *Audiobook Player*—Karl was able to tolerate transitioning into the restroom and completed his hygiene tasks successfully. Today, Karl is independent for toileting, thanks to Shrek and Edgar Allan Poe!

BOB BOOKS #1 - READING MAGIC

by Learning Touch

http://learningtouch.com/products

$1.99 (iPhone) $3.99 (iPad)

Sam had a cat.

FROM THE DEVELOPER

Start your child reading with this phonics-based interactive game. The simple drag-and-drop interface can be used by the youngest children. Your favorite *Bob Books* characters and full-color animations encourage kids along the path of learning to read.

CUSTOMER REVIEW

Your child can develop a love for reading with *Bob Books*. This app is not only a student favorite, but a tried and true learn-to-read teaching method. *Bob Books* add just the right amount of student interaction with instruction and colorful animations to keep beginning readers focused and motivated for extended periods of time. The *Bob Books* app uses the same learning methods and principles as the bestselling *Bob Books* series. The *Bob Books* app slowly introduces new letter sounds using consistency, repetition, and stories that make learning to read and spell fun for all. Try the free version and you will be hooked on *Bob Books*.

STARFALL ABCS

by Starfall Education

http://more.starfall.com/info/apps/starfall-education.php

$2.99

FROM THE DEVELOPER

Children delight as they see, hear, and interact with letters and sounds in words, sentences, and games. They learn to recognize letters and develop phonics skills that will ensure they become confident readers.

* *Starfall*™ is a registered trademark. © (1/2011) Starfall Education, reproduced with permission.

CUSTOMER REVIEW

Finally, my favorite website (starfall.com) is available on an app. My colleagues and I use *Starfall* on a daily basis to teach not only reading skills, but computer literacy, labeling, phonics, following directions, etc. I have not met a student who did not become instantly enchanted with *Starfall*, and now I can put it on my portable device to make *Starfall* more accessible than ever. *Starfall ABCs* (app) and starfall.com (website) are highly recommended technology to build literacy in all students, on the desktop and on the go.

 Starfall ABCs does not have the content of the entire website. Only the ABC portion of the website is included in the app. We all sincerely hope that Starfall Education produces the entire reading series in app format soon.

SEE READ SAY

by 2BPM Software

www.2bpmsoftware.com/srs

$0.99

FROM THE DEVELOPER

Confidence and reading ability improve when children know Dolch sight words, many of which are in almost anything they read. Readers will have more experiences of success if they know these words. Dolch words are service words, which are necessary for understanding sentences.

CUSTOMER REVIEW

The *See Read Say* app features talking flashcards for all 220 Dolch sight words. Good practice for students learning to read. The graphics are beautiful and the audio is good. There is no verbal praise, cheering, or clapping; however, there is a star-based scoring system that keeps students motivated.

 The tracking system included in *See Read Say* that counts the number of words completed is not necessarily accurate. Be watchful if using tracking information as data.

K-3 SIGHT WORDS

by Eric Kitter

http://ksw.kitter.info/Kindergarten_Sight_Words.html

$0.99

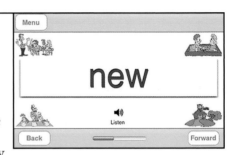

FROM THE DEVELOPER

Reading is the most important skill a child will ever have. In most schools, children are expected to be able to read short stories by the end of the first grade. Many of the words cannot be sounded out; they have to be memorized. A list of words called the "Dolch Sight Words" was compiled to help children memorize the most important words needed to be able to achieve this task.

CUSTOMER REVIEW

K-3 Sight Words is a "no glamour" app. The user simply files through the flashcards by pressing the forward or backward buttons. If you need help with the word, the Listen button will say the word for you. *K-3 Sight Words* is a fun alternative to tag board flashcards.

SIGHT WORDS CIRCUS - 300 SIGHTWORDS

by App-Zoo

http://app-zoo.com

$0.99

FROM THE DEVELOPER

Sight words made fun. You have to see it to believe it! (free version available) Is *believe* a sight word?

CUSTOMER REVIEW

If your child or student enjoys the bells and whistles of getting correct answers, *Sight Words Circus* is the app for them. Dancing words and letters combined with music make this app rousing for individuals who are challenged by sight words. Both graphics and audio are very good. With *Sight Words Circus*, the user has the option of viewing a complete list of grade level words (Review Show) or practicing one word at a time (Watch Show). The user also has the option to flag words for extra practice. Words are grouped in grade levels from pre-primer to third grade. *Sight Words Circus* is recommended for students who need a little extra motivation to stay focused.

DR. SEUSS'S ABC

by Oceanhouse Media

www.oceanhousemedia.com/products/abc

$3.99

FROM THE DEVELOPER

New features available only in these eBooks include professional narration, background audio, and enlarged artwork for each scene. To promote reading in young children, individual words are highlighted as the story is read. By combining the original text and artwork of Dr. Seuss with features that entertain and promote reading, this eBook appeals to readers of all ages.

CUSTOMER REVIEW

You can trust Dr. Seuss to deliver quality. *Dr. Seuss's ABC* is just one of the many quality apps available from Oceanhouse Media. Each eBook features three modes of reading: read to me, read it myself, and auto play. As the user reads through the book, he or she can touch a picture to have a zoom-up of the word spoken and then attach it to the picture. *Dr. Seuss's ABC* is highly recommended for beginning readers.

Also suggested:

| The Lorax | The Cat in the Hat | Green Eggs and Ham | How the Grinch Stole Christmas! | Yertle the Turtle |

SHREK FOREVER AFTER KID'S BOOK HD & HOW TO TRAIN YOUR DRAGON KID'S BOOK HD & NATE'S BIG HAIR KIDS BOOK

by FrogDogMedia

www.istorytimeapp.com

$2.99 each (Shrek & Dragon) or $0.99 (Big Hair)

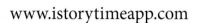

FROM THE DEVELOPER

Welcome to *iStoryTime*, a library of narrated children's books for the iPhone. *iStoryTime* books are illustrated and narrated, so your child can enjoy the book even when you're busy. Best of all, the app is drop-dead simple to use because it's actually designed for kids aged two years and up.

CUSTOMER REVIEW

iStoryTime books are masterfully executed with beautiful graphics and clear, articulate audio. *iStoryTime* provides the user with options to read by one's self or to be read to by others. And, if turning the page (swiping) is a challenge, *iStoryTime* books will automatically turn the pages for you. According to the National Education Association (NEA), "Motivating children to read is an important factor in student achievement and creating lifelong successful readers. Research has shown that children who are motivated and spend more time reading do better in school." *iStoryTime* books are recommended for everyone at every ability level. iTherapy opportunities include labeling, describing, finger isolation, eye-hand coordination, sequencing, and visual integration; Social pragmatic skills also will be enhanced.

TOY STORY READ-ALONG

by Disney Publishing Worldwide

http://disneydigitalbooks.go.com/?cmp=ddb_hp_redirect_extl

FREE

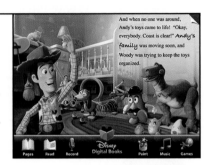

FROM THE DEVELOPER

"To Infinity and beyond!" *Toy Story Read-Along* takes you on the adventure of a lifetime: It is a fully interactive reading experience packed with games, movie clips, coloring pages, sing-along tunes, and surprises on every page. Hear the story read aloud, record your own narration, or explore at your own pace.

CUSTOMER REVIEW

Toy Story Read-Along is one of the best free apps I have encountered. Students can read it themselves, record their voices, or have it read to them with great audio. *Toy Story Read-Along* includes games, music, and interactive activities that keep my students engaged with excellent screen display and 3D-like animation.

 There is a similar app, *Toy Story 3* (free version), that is merely an advertisement for the higher priced Toy Story apps.

AUDIOBOOK PLAYER - 2300 FREE AUDIOBOOKS

by Alex Sokirynsky

http://audiobookplayer.net

$2.99

FROM THE DEVELOPER

Enjoy thousands of free classic audio books!

CUSTOMER REVIEW

Audiobook Player–2300 Free Audiobooks is a splendid resource for anyone who has difficulty with reading, vision, or visual perception challenges. *Audiobook Player* lets individuals enjoy a good book on their own terms. Books can be fast-forwarded, rewound, bookmarked, and downloaded one chapter at a time. Consider the free version, *Audiobook Player–FREE*, if you like your books one at a time. The free version limits the user to one book at a time. No more clunky recorders, cassette tapes, extra large headphones, or restricted choices for visually/reading challenged individuals. My young adult students who would not otherwise be exposed to the classics are quoting books, titles, authors, and phrases from classics like *Tom Sawyer*, *The Secret Garden*, and "The Cask of Amontillado." Everyone loves a good book!

Chapter 23: Spelling

Focusing on spelling is important, because poor spelling can hamper writing and convey negative impressions. Individuals who are unable to use verbal language may express themselves via letter blocks, writing, or keyboarding. Let's make sure they can spell.

MONTESSORI CROSSWORDS - TEACH AND LEARN SPELLING WITH FUN PUZZLES FOR CHILDREN

by L'Escapadou

http://lescapadou.com/LEscapadou_-_Fun_and_Educational_applications_for_iPad_and_IPhone/Montessori_Crosswords.html

$1.99

FROM THE DEVELOPER

This is the only app that offers a fun, interactive game to help kids develop their reading, writing, and spelling skills using the proven Montessori method of learning, and 300 different word-picture-audio combinations and letters sounds (phonics)!

CUSTOMER REVIEW

The Montessori Method is an educational approach based on the research of educator Maria Montessori that supports the natural development of children. *Montessori Crosswords* is brilliant, as it encourages students to explore reading, writing, spelling, and fine motor activities with compelling visual effects and soothing audio soundtracks. There are three levels of difficulty and each level supplies the user with a prompt, if needed. There is even a moveable alphabet that can rotate, change size, and produce the sound of the letter when touched. There are letter case, layout, and audio choices for the user to customize their preferences. Also included is a word count; however, it cannot be reset for multiple users.

SPELL BLOCKS WITH SIGHT WORDS

by 2BPM Software

www.2bpmsoftware.com

$0.99

FROM THE DEVELOPER

Your child will learn over 200 Dolch Sight Words by spelling each one after it is spoken to them. *Spell Blocks* says the word and offers the scrambled letter choices to choose from. Your child then touches and moves each letter to its correct place.

CUSTOMER REVIEW

Hear the sight word spoken (not great audio) and then click and drag the letter blocks into the correct order to spell the words. Make it more challenging by adding extra letters. With *Spell Blocks*, you can choose the level that is right for your needs, pre-primer to third grade. Words can be flagged as they are mastered. *Spell Blocks* will track data/proficiency to keep track of your student. This feature is great for parents or educators tracking a child; however, it is not for teachers who need to track many students.

WORD MAGIC & DICTATION & SIGHT WORDS AND DIGRAPHS

by anusen.com

www.anusen.com

$0.99 each (*Word Magic* & *Dictation*) or $0.99 (*Sight Words*)

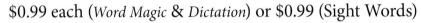

FROM THE DEVELOPER

In *Word Magic*, a picture is shown with its accompanying word; Users then select the missing letter in the word. When completed, the word is read aloud. There are three flavors: Based on the child's level, you can choose to have the missing letter at the beginning, in the middle, or at the end of the word. *Dictation* helps children learn and remember word spellings easily, providing a simple way of combining audio and pictures.

The *Sight Words and Digraphs* application is designed keeping preschoolers in mind. It is ideal for kids between the ages three to eight. It is an excellent application for kids to have fun with words and their spellings. This application will help kids to learn and identify sight words and digraphs.

CUSTOMER REVIEW

All three apps are designed by Anusen. If your goal is to increase sight words and spelling, then this set of apps will support your student. Unfortunately, there is not a free version for trial. My colleagues and I have had both good and disinterested reviews from our students.

 As a speech-language pathologist, I would suggest that the audio be cleaner, with more precise articulation. My students sometimes have difficulty understanding the audio.

Chapter 24: Math

As with reading disabilities, when math difficulties are present, they can range from mild to severe. Many students have persistent trouble memorizing basic facts in all four operations (addition, subtraction, multiplication, and division), despite great efforts to do so. Providing individuals with visual supports to mathematical equations could be your answer.

KIDCALC 7-IN-1 MATH FUN

by Steve Glinberg

http://kidcalc.wordpress.com

$0.99

FROM THE DEVELOPER

KidCalc includes animated addition, subtraction, multiplication, and division lessons. *KidCalc* is easily configured to adjust the "challenge level" of counting and math puzzles. Settings vary for toddlers learning numbers, for preschoolers learning to add and subtract, and for elementary school-aged kids learning to count as high as 1,000 and to multiply and divide.

CUSTOMER REVIEW

KidCalc is super cute and super fun. Many of my students will use this app as a reinforcer. Students who have had difficulty with math concepts for years are finally motivated and making connections. *KidCalc* is easily individualized for every ability level and fun themes make it topical for different times of the year. The developer adds holiday and seasonal themes throughout the year. Great price! Great app! Even the audio is clear and articulate.

123 ANIMALS COUNTING HD - FOR iPAD

by Brain Counts

www.braincounts.com/BrainGames/123AnimalsCounting.aspx

$1.99

FROM THE DEVELOPER

123 Animals Counting HD–for iPad teaches toddlers and young kids visually and vocally how to count with fun, animated animals and touch screen interaction.

CUSTOMER REVIEW

123 Animals Counting is great for individuals learning how to count or mastering one-to-one correspondence. The user does not need to know how to read as *123 Animals Counting* has a voice-over option. The audio and reinforcement system are appealing to younger students. Students can count along with the app (verbal and graphic) as they touch each animal. Listening skills are developed by hearing the names of the animal and the sound associated with the animal. Try the free sample version before you decide to buy.

TIME, MONEY & FRACTIONS ON-TRACK

by School Zone Publishing

www.schoolzone.com

$9.99

FROM THE DEVELOPER

Learning about time, money, and fractions can be challenging for many children. School Zone's *Time, Money & Fractions On-Track* app for the iPad is the perfect tool to help children build those skills! The program's kid-friendly approach delivers solid practice that will build confidence and help children succeed in school.

CUSTOMER REVIEW

Time, Money & Fractions On-Track offers great visual supports for students on the spectrum. General education teachers use and recommend this app. *Time, Money & Fractions On-Track* has students moving hands on a clock, handling money, and dividing color pies to learn fractions. Games and reinforcement are incorporated into the app to provide students with a break and keep them interested. The progress-tracking section should be more detailed. This app is well worth the cost if you are targeting the concepts of time, money, or fractions. I know teachers who bought similar DVDs for six times that amount of money.

ROCKET MATH

by Dan Russell-Pinson

http://dan-russell-pinson.com/blog/games-rocket-math.asp

$0.99

FROM THE DEVELOPER

While your rocket is floating weightlessly in space, the real fun begins! Play one of the 56 different math missions. Each mission has touchable objects floating in space, including stars, coins, clocks, 3D shapes, and even pizzas! Earn a bronze, silver, or gold medal and also try to beat your high score. Missions range in difficulty from even/odd numbers all the way to square roots, so kids and their parents will enjoy hours of fun while learning math.

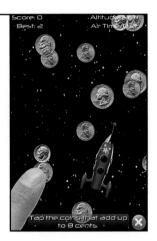

CUSTOMER REVIEW

Choose your rocket, choose your avatar, and begin your mathematical mission with *Rocket Math*! Earn medals and money to design your space machine and send it on a quest. There are 56 different math missions from counting to square roots. Features include rocket parts, sound effects, three difficulty levels, 15 avatars, and up to five player profiles.

 Auditory processing skills should be adequate to follow one-step directions. There are many layers to this game and some students can get overwhelmed by sound effects and the quick pace. Some may require adult coaching to become familiar with the settings.

MATH MAGIC & MATH SERIES

by anusen.com

www.anusen.com

$0.99 each

↘ FROM THE DEVELOPER

Your child will improve in adding, subtracting, multiplying, and dividing with *Math Magic*. You never get tired of hearing, "Can I do math?" from your six-year-old, do you? Of course you don't. *Math Series* is designed with preschoolers and kindergarten kids in mind. Ideal for kids between the ages three and eight, it is an excellent application for kids to have fun with numbers and math.

CUSTOMER REVIEW

Classroom teachers have been using *Math Magic* to help fight the boredom of traditional flashcards and dittos. Teachers are reporting that students will participate in math goals willingly, so student interest improves as well as knowledge. Especially useful is the "Magic Wand" feature for addition and subtraction.

 The audio is difficult to understand. The volume is unstable and the articulation is unclear. Anusen, please fix this. *Math Series* is exactly what the name suggests, a series of numbers with one blank space. The user fills in the blank from a choice of four. If your goal is to fill in the missing number from a number line, this is your app.

MATH CARDS

by DollarApp

www.dollarapp.com/apps

$0.99

FROM THE DEVELOPER

Math Cards offers quick quizzes in basic math for the iPhone and iPod touch. Students will improve math skills with these simple, built-in lessons. The number of correctly-answered questions is displayed as both a letter grade and in percentages.

CUSTOMER REVIEW

Math Cards has no sound or reward system, but the quick-touch response system and the touch-and-hold for additional feedback feature are great for reinforcement. These are simple flash cards for math practice. Choose from addition, subtraction, division, and multiplication.

MATH FLASH CARDS

by One Moxie Ventures LLC

www.onemoxie.com/education/math-flash-cards

$0.99

FROM THE DEVELOPER

Math Flash Cards is a fun-to-use math drill app that looks and works just like paper flash cards. Great for kids and parents to practice and refresh arithmetic skills. Boost your memory and brain using *Math Flash Cards*.

CUSTOMER REVIEW

The "no glamour" *Math Flash Cards* app is perfect for individuals who need to develop basic math skills. Teachers and parents like this app because they can customize quizzes and set the number of cards per drill. I like this app because it tracks data and time. If you need math practice without distraction, this is the app for you.

JUMBO CALCULATOR

by Christopher Weems

http://christopherweems.com/iphone

FREE

FROM THE DEVELOPER

Jumbo Calculator is great for anyone wanting the ease-of-use of a large-buttoned calculator. While, sadly, you can't feel the exquisite texture of its large plastic buttons, and the virtual solar panel doesn't actually charge, *Jumbo Calculator* succeeds at its main purpose: adding, subtracting, multiplying, dividing, squaring, and square-rooting. One size fits all.

CUSTOMER REVIEW

What you see is what you get. *Jumbo Calculator* is perfect for individuals with vision or motor difficulties. This is a straightforward, large-button calculator, for free.

Chapter 25: Preschool

Students with disabilities are not always given the opportunity and time necessary to become familiar with the key words and concepts that are the building blocks of future schooling. With a trend toward more inclusive educational experiences for all children with disabilities, we should give them every opportunity to succeed and meet their goals. Children with disabilities as young as three years old are using preschool apps to get a jumpstart on their education.

Success Story: Ethan

Because many of the preschool applications use a multiple choice format, Ethan is able to show he knows his letters, colors, and shapes (age-appropriate skills for a four-year-old) even to those who have difficulty understanding his speech. Same-age peers find it cool and love to take turns with Ethan, which is a whole other level of learning. He is able to be fairly independent and once we get him to the game, he wants to play. He is able to click on answers easily and is even beginning to get the hang of dragging items, which has been a major roadblock to using a computer mouse. We love that it is infinitely patient with him and that skills can be presented multiple ways to help with reinforcement and generalization. We like to use it while waiting in restaurants or at the doctor's office and in the car because it is small. The biggest problem we've run into is trying to take it away before he is finished!

—Beth Ann Bourne, Ethan's mom

Ethan mastering preschool con-

cepts on his iPod touch

SUPER WHY!

by PBS KIDS

http://pbskids.org/mobile

$2.99

FROM THE DEVELOPER

Help your child achieve the "Power to Read" with this collection of four *SUPER WHY!* interactive literacy games. Your child can play along with each of the four main characters from the TV series—Alpha Pig, Princess Presto, Wonder Red, and, of course, SUPER WHY—while practicing the alphabet, rhyming, spelling, writing, and reading. Super Duper!

CUSTOMER REVIEW

SUPER WHY! is super cute. This was Zach's first app (see "Zach's a Mac" in the Introduction). At three and a half years of age, he began learning pre-reading skills with *SUPER WHY!* and an iPad. If you are a beginning reader with good auditory processing skills, this is the app for you. Each character gives the user instructions on how to proceed through the game. While they are cute, they talk a lot, which is too much for my students who have auditory processing challenges. The audio and graphics are outstanding.

 There is no Settings page. The user cannot make choices regarding music, sound effects, or voices.

GAME FACTORY HD

by Bacciz

http://bacciz.com

$0.99

Game Factory HD helps your child develop memory, cognitive, motor, speech, and language skills while having fun! *Game Factory HD* features:

- 4 fun educational games

- 5 cool match themes!

- 6 different language combinations:

  English, German, French, Spanish, Japanese, and Chinese!

- 5 difficulty levels: perfect for kids of all ages!

Excellent customization features allow you to upload pictures of mom, dad, grandparents, and friends and see them interact within the games. Rated number 2 in the Education category and by Apple iTunes as a Staff Favorite!

CUSTOMER REVIEW

If you are learning your ABCs, 123s, shapes, animals, a foreign language, or trying to reach an individual goal, this is the app for you! I recommend turning the music off; it can be distracting. *Game Factory HD* keeps track of scores, but does not capture data. My favorite part of this app is the ability to customize to student goals.

ABC TRACER - ALPHABET FLASHCARD TRACING PHONICS AND DRAWING

by App-Zoo

http://app-zoo.com

$1.99

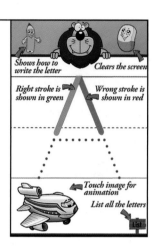

FROM THE DEVELOPER

ABC Tracer teaches kids how to write. It:

- animates and shows users how to write letters with demonstrated strokes, in the right order, on traditional red-blue guiding lines.

- provides fun feedback for strokes made correctly and incorrectly.

- has lots of fun activities!

  - Touching the image below the letter makes it come to life!

  - The Drawing screen features fun music.

  - Pop the randomly arranged balloons in alphabetical order!

CUSTOMER REVIEW

ABC Tracer is so motivating, I have had students who strongly dislike pencil-and-paper work sit and work for extended periods of time forming letters. Letter formation, motor planning, eye-hand coordination, and immediate feedback make this app tremendously popular with occupational therapists. The audio is tinny-sounding; however, the students like it. Who's complaining?

MONKEY PRESCHOOL LUNCHBOX

by THUP Games

www.monkeypreschool.com

$0.99

FROM THE DEVELOPER

Learn and have fun by helping monkeys pack their lunch!
Monkey Preschool Lunchbox is a collection of six exciting
educational games. Six different games teach kids about
colors, letters, counting, shapes, sizes, matching, and differences.

CUSTOMER REVIEW

Monkey Preschool Lunchbox targets a variety of concepts and fine motor control with
fun puzzles and activities. A student can even earn stickers. Usually, no instruction is
required and students are engaged. *Monkey Preschool Lunchbox* has no settings and the
questions are randomized. Many of my students will work to earn time on *Monkey Preschool Lunchbox*. Work to Work: I like it!

SHAPE BUILDER - THE PRESCHOOL LEARNING PUZZLE GAME

by Darren Murtha Design

http://touchscreenpreschoolgames.com/support

$0.99

FROM THE DEVELOPER

Shape Builder educates & entertains your little one with easy-to-move shapes that snap into place on top of silhouette puzzles. Each puzzle has five to ten pieces and after positioning all of the pieces, the real image is revealed along with a professional voice recording of the word.

CUSTOMER REVIEW

Build confidence and an "I can" attitude with *Shape Builder*. Learn numbers, letters, and nouns while strengthening fine motor skills by assembling shapes into a colorful puzzle. When the puzzle is complete, the image and written word are revealed to reinforce participation and learning.

 All puzzles are random; therefore individual goals cannot be targeted.

FEED ME!

by Edutainment Resources, Inc.

www.pencilbot.com/feedme/feedme/Feed_Me.html

FREE

FROM THE DEVELOPER

PencilBot–Kids' *Feed Me!* is a series developed by teachers and parents who love to make learning fun! This simple, easy-to-use game can be enjoyed by children and their parents as they play along. Feed the little monster the correct "food" he is thinking of and unlock trophies for your trophy case! Feed the monster the wrong item and he might get sick. But don't worry; you'll have the chance to try the question again later in the game.

CUSTOMER REVIEW

Feed Me! covers a variety of language concepts. Unfortunately, they are not categorized. The cute purple Monster thinks of a question (letter recognition, shapes, vocabulary, spelling or math) and the user is required to feed the monster the right answer. The voiceover is a clear, articulate child's voice. *Feed Me!* is engaging for the students; however, the educator or caregiver cannot focus on a specific goal. A benefit of *Feed Me!* is the fact that it comes in seven languages. I recommend giving it a try. It is free and can be deleted if your child or student does not enjoy it.

 When feeding the monster, the food/answer has to be put directly into his mouth. This has frustrated some of my students; however, it does provide an entertaining format for learning basic concepts and strengthens fine motor skills. It's free, so you decide.

ALPHABET FUN!

by John Cotant

www.tapfuze.com

$2.99

FROM THE DEVELOPER

Alphabet Fun is like having preschool right on your iPad! Filled with over 50 full-color images and large, easy-to-read text, *Alphabet Fun* provides an excellent platform for preschoolers.

CUSTOMER REVIEW

Give your child a jump on preschool with *Alphabet Fun*. Your child will have the opportunity to hear, write, and say their numbers, ABCs, colors, and whole words on their iDevice. Both audio and graphics are lively and engaging for the young, and young at heart. Recommended for anyone mastering basic preschool concepts.

 The developer is promising "great new features."

Part VIII

Neurological Communication Disorders (dysarthria, aphasia, apraxia, and dysphagia)

Communication is necessary for the positive health of human beings. When affected negatively, it may alter individuals' lives and cause them to be socially withdrawn. Whether congenital or acquired, neurological communication disorders can be devastating. There are several classifications of neurological disorders that may cause individuals to lose their ability to understand, speak, chew, and swallow. I will focus on four of those disorders in this section. I strongly recommend using the apps in this section under the guidance of a speech-language pathologist. While none will cause any ill effects, proper and consistent use can lead to extraordinary results.

iPad Could Be a Beneficial Device for the Disabled

—by RedOrbit

When it comes to high-tech gadgets like the iPad, most people see a sleek, multi-media entertainment platform, but Professor Gregg Vanderheiden sees other potential possibilities for the Apple touch-screen device.

Vanderheiden, director of the Trace Research and Development Center at the University of Wisconsin at Madison, says the iPad could be an important tool for people with speech problems and other disabilities.

"Say you have somebody who's had a stroke, for example, and they wake up and they can't communicate … Instead of buying a 5,000-dollar communications aid you take out your iPad and download an app and—bam!—they can communicate," he told AFP.

The Trace Center helps those who are unable to speak and cannot communicate properly, and researchers from the center, including Vanderheiden, are excited about the potential the iPad is showing for a relatively low-cost communication tool.

Karen Sheehan, the executive director of the Alliance for Technology Access, a California-based group that looks for ways to expand technology to allow those with disabilities to live better qualitative lives, said there is much interest in the iPad.

People with autism, spinal injuries, cerebral palsy or ALS, and stroke victims could all possibly benefit from the iPad: "Anyone who's nonverbal and needs a device to speak for them," said Sheehan.

There are many useful communication tools available for helping those with disabilities, "but they tend to run into the thousands of dollars, which can be prohibitive for a lot of people," said Sheehan. The iPad can be turned into a very inexpensive communication tool that does the same job as many of the more expensive medical devices.

AssistiveWare is one company that has adapted communication applications for the iPhone and iPod touch. Their *Proloquo2Go* app has been revamped to also work with the iPad and is available at Apple's App Store for less than $200.

Proloquo2Go works by allowing users who have difficulty speaking to communicate using symbols to represent phrases. They can also type in what they want to say and the words can be converted to speech using text-to-speech technology with a natural sounding voice.

The iPad's large screen makes it more useful to a wider range of people than the iPhone and iPod touch, said Sheehan. "They've such a small area and for someone who has limited fine motor it's hard to hit small icons . . . It's easier on the iPad to just click on an icon to say 'I want juice,' or 'I want to watch a movie.'"

Joanne Castellano, Director of the New Jersey-based TechConnection, which provides "assistive technology" solutions to people with disabilities, said that the iPad seems like a very useful tool and although the touch-screen controls are part of the attraction of the gadget, it could prove to be a challenge for some people with disabilities.

"The way you have to pinch some things with your thumb and your forefinger—that movement might be a problem for some people," she said. "But to turn the page of a book you just have to swipe it, so that could be very helpful."

Dan Herlihy of Connective Technology Solutions told AFP he planned on getting the iPad to use with other tools he utilizes to address the needs of people with disabilities. "And I can already think of about half a dozen things I'll run on it," he said.

Vanderheiden said the iPad is a "great platform—small, inexpensive, a lot of power, a long battery," but its greatest contribution to the needs of the disabled may be from the applications built for the device.

"They offer the opportunity for just tremendous, unprecedented innovation."

RedOrbit.com is the premier Internet destination for space, science, health, and technology enthusiasts around the globe.

Chapter 26: Dysphagia

Dysphagia is the only disorder where a speech-language pathologist can affect an individual's physical health. People with dysphagia have difficulty swallowing, which makes it difficult to take in enough calories and fluids for nourishment. Dysphagia can lead to aspiration of food or liquids and ultimately pneumonia. A qualified speech pathologist can design an exercise program and provide compensatory techniques that can significantly reduce the risk of choking and aspiration.

SMALLTALK DYSPHAGIA

by Lingraphica

www.aphasia.com

FREE

FROM THE DEVELOPER

SmallTalk Dysphagia contains 50 phrases covering eating equipment, meal assistance, diet, liquids, medications, and compensatory treatment techniques. It also contains four demonstration videos of treatment techniques commonly used for swallowing.

CUSTOMER REVIEW

It has been years since I worked in a hospital setting. We would scribble notes and tape them on the headboards hoping the overworked staff would follow through. And now, there is an app for that. *SmallTalk Dysphagia* has every compensatory technique available with short, easy-to-follow demonstration videos, clear icons, and good audio (male or female). If only I could select, print, and post or file the most important techniques, equipment, and supports to fit individual needs. Icons and videos can be rearranged and deleted as necessary. Highly recommended for individuals with dysphagia and their caregivers.

SMALLTALK ORAL MOTOR EXERCISES

by Lingraphica

www.aphasia.com

FREE

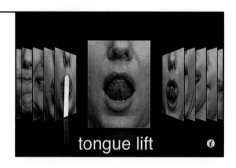

tongue lift

FROM THE DEVELOPER

Designed for people with weak mouth, tongue, and lip muscles and/or poor oral coordination, SmallTalk oral motor exercises are videos illustrating cheek, tongue, palate, lip, and jaw movements that help strengthen the oral musculature.

CUSTOMER REVIEW

Fantastic! *SmallTalk Oral Motor Exercises* is just the best tool a speech pathologist could ask for. *SmallTalk* costs less than flashcards and provides the instructions and motivation needed for independent practice throughout the day. Videos and instructions are clear and precise with no distractions. My secret joy is that I will not have to do oral motor exercises while counting and demonstrating again. All 50 exercises are easy to access with a swipe of the finger. Exercises can be repeated again and again for focused rehabilitation.

 Seek the advice of a physician and speech pathologist prior to starting any treatments. Oral motor exercises can compound certain medical conditions.

Chapter 27: Aphasia, Apraxia & Dysarthria

The oral motor exercises and speech activities presented in the following apps are used by trained speech pathologists. Now they can be put in your pocket, purse, or pack, and used anytime!

VAST™-AUTISM 1-CORE

by SpeakinMotion™

www.proactivespeechtherapy.com (for further information on Autism 1- Core)

www.speakinmotion.com (for further information on *SpeakinMotion*)

$4.99

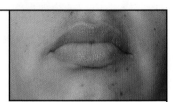

FROM THE DEVELOPER

I designed this app to work for individuals who have motor speech challenges and/or autism after seeing how extremely effective the VAST technique is with adult acquired apraxia and non-fluent aphasia. My colleagues and I have had amazing results with students on the spectrum as well as students with motor speech programming disorders.

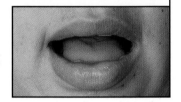

CUSTOMER REVIEW

VAST™-Autism 1-Core provides unprecedented support for spoken language, combining evidence-based best practices and technology to deliver remarkable results.

VAST™-Autism 1-Core is a groundbreaking tool that provides state-of-the-art therapy to students with autism and motor speech programming disorders such as apraxia. *VAST™-Autism 1-Core* combines the highly effective concept of video modeling with written words and auditory cues to help individuals acquire relevant words, phrases, and sentences so that they can speak for themselves. For children and individuals with strong visual skills, this can be a key to developing speech.

VAST™ AUTISM 1-CORE (continued)

Videos are organized into a hierarchy of five categories beginning with syllables and ending with sentences. Each video gives a spoken target utterance that is preceded by the written word(s). Each word, phrase and sentence is concrete and has meaning that can be generalized and practiced throughout the day. Providing the written word will prevent a student from labeling a picture of a frog jumping as "go," a person lying on a mat as "break time" or labeling a swing as "weee." The ability to recognize the written target word(s) will increase functional communication and enhance acquisition of spoken language. The progression of *VAST™-Autism 1-Core* Videos is as follows:

1. Syllable Repetition

2. Single Syllable Words

3. Multi-Syllabic Words

4. Phrases

5. Sentences

SMALLTALK APHASIA & SMALLTALK COMMON PHRASES

by Lingraphica

www.aphasia.com

FREE

FROM THE DEVELOPER

SmallTalk Common Phrases and *SmallTalk Aphasia* apps provide a series of speech-exercise videos, each illustrating the tongue and lip movements necessary to produce a commonly used short phrase in everyday vocabulary. With this app, people with apraxia, aphasia, and/or dysarthria resulting from stroke or head injury can easily practice commonly used phrases and repeat each one as often as they like.

CUSTOMER REVIEW

The SmallTalk app series is excellent! I have searched for video clips of the articulators for many years. Both *SmallTalk Common Phrases* and *SmallTalk Aphasia* provide the user with clear audio, graphics, text, and video of common phrases. *SmallTalk Aphasia* has an additional icons feature, which provides common phrases in written and graphic form. The SmallTalk series was originally meant for adults with aphasia; however, they work fabulously with students on the spectrum and/or students with apraxia. SmallTalk apps provide video modeling for speech. I would also like to note that an iPad, iPod touch, or iPhone are superb companions and time killers for individuals in the hospital. Now, these same iDevices can also communicate important medical information. I highly recommended SmallTalk apps for individuals with apraxia, aphasia, dysarthria, and autism of all ages.

SPEAKINMOTION TRIAL

by NexStar Consulting

www.speakinmotion.com

FREE

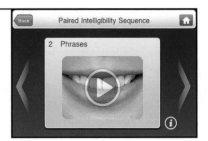

↘ FROM THE DEVELOPER

SpeakinMotion on the iPhone delivers a mobile VAST™ solution—providing specialized therapy and functional video to help communicatively impaired individuals speak for themselves. VAST is an innovative application of video technology to facilitate and improve communication abilities for speech-impaired individuals (usually as a result of stroke or traumatic brain injury). Following a close-up video of mouth movements allows these individuals to speak full sentences. The simultaneous combination of visual, auditory, and in some cases, written cues, allows these individuals to readily produce speech.

↘ CUSTOMER REVIEW

SpeakinMotion Trial is an introductory app that allows the user to follow along with mouth movements on a pre-recorded video. *SpeakinMotion* was developed to support individuals with acquired apraxia and/or aphasia; however, it is just what I need for my students with apraxia, motor speech, and hearing-based challenges. The Trial app gives the user an introductory set of generic videos for therapeutic and functional communication.

 The developers are motivated to provide additional videos that will support users with everyday needs. *SpeakinMotion* is FREE. Give it a try and don't forget to take a look at the getting started section.

SMALLTALK LETTERS, NUMBERS, COLORS

by Lingraphica

www.aphasia.com

FREE

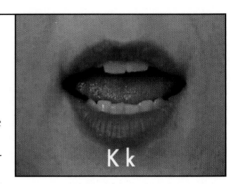

FROM THE DEVELOPER

The *SmallTalk Letters, Numbers, Colors* app provides a series of speech-exercise videos, each illustrating the tongue and lip movements necessary to produce a single color, number, or letter. With this app, people with apraxia, aphasia, and/or dysarthria resulting from stroke or head injury can easily practice individual colors, numbers, or letters as often as they like.

CUSTOMER REVIEW

SmallTalk Letters, Numbers, Colors was developed to help folks who have had strokes or head injury practice tongue and lip movements to produce single words. My colleagues in the hospitals tell me that SmallTalk apps work incredibly well with those scenarios. I use *Letters, Numbers, Colors* with my students on the spectrum and/or with apraxia and they work equally fabulously. One young man was so excited by the video modeling he spent a whole afternoon filing through letters, numbers, and colors until it was time to go home. The next session, he began repeating after the video model. Success. Recommended for anyone who has apraxia, motor planning challenges, or depends upon visual input for success.

SMALLTALK PHONEMES &
SMALLTALK CONSONANT BLENDS
by Lingraphica

www.aphasia.com

FREE

FROM THE DEVELOPER

SmallTalk Phonemes and *SmallTalk Consonant Blends* provide a series of speech-exercise videos, each illustrating the tongue and lip movements necessary to produce a single phoneme and single consonant blend. With this app, people with apraxia, aphasia, and/or dysarthria resulting from stroke or head injury can easily practice the specific phonemes they need and repeat them as often as they like.

CUSTOMER REVIEW

SmallTalk phonemes and *SmallTalk Consonant Blends* are tools that every speech therapist should have access to. Video Modeling provides an effective method of teaching new skills, particularly if an individual avoids face-to-face interactions and can readily processes visual information. SmallTalk articulation series is highly recommended for individuals of all ages who have difficulty producing single phonemes or consonant blends.

Part IX

Stuttering

According to the Stuttering Foundation, stuttering is a communication disorder in which the flow of speech is broken by repetitions (li-li-like this), prolongations (lllllike this), or abnormal stoppages (no sound) of sounds and syllables. There may also be unusual facial and body movements associated with the effort to speak. Stuttering is also referred to as stammering.

Chapter 28: Stuttering

Stuttering and the iPod, iPad, iPhone: The Need for Technology Use Has Always Been There

—by Barbara Fernandes M.S; CCC-SLP

As a graduate student, I was assigned to a client with concerns regarding his fluency skills. He was 28 years old at that time, and in the therapy process we were trying to address not only verbal fluency, but also the underlying issues associated with his stuttering: One of them was his avoidance behaviors, as well as his feelings associated with his stuttering. My supervisor asked me to create a form that he would have to fill out daily with information regarding his feelings towards his speech as well as the moments that he avoided a specific situation due to the fear of stuttering.

After working with him for one semester, he never turned in any of the weekly forms that I provided for him. As a therapist, I had the intention of checking for carryover and positive attitude towards speaking; however, I cannot blame my client for not carrying a piece of paper with him around town to write down his avoidance moments or feelings associated with his speech. He was in business school, and while he told me he did not do it because he was too busy, he later confessed that it was inconvenient to fill out the papers throughout the day, and by night he would forget how he felt during the day.

That's when I had the idea of a possible "device" that the client would have with him at all times. What could it be? How about his own phone? That is exactly how the *Fluency Tracker* app was born. *Fluency Tracker* is not only convenient and more discreet than pencil-and-paper methods for the person who stutters, but also for the speech therapist because it provides a graph of the changes in fluency behavior over time.

Fluency Tracker is also very convenient for parents as they become active participants in their child's treatment by tracking it outside of the speech therapist's office. It also provides excellent visual data by displaying a graph of the person's progress over time.

FLUENCY TRACKER

by Smarty Ears

http://smartyearsapps.com/2010/10/26/fluency-tracker

$9.99

↘ FROM THE DEVELOPER

Fluency Tracker is an application designed for individuals who stutter and parents of children who stutter. *Fluency Tracker* will complement the services of speech therapists in making progress toward more fluent speech, positive feelings about speech, and reducing avoidance behaviors that are associated with stuttering.

↘ CUSTOMER REVIEW

My colleagues who specialize in stuttering tell me that *Fluency Tracker* is helpful in carryover and generalization of skills practiced in the therapy setting. *Fluency Tracker* brings data from natural situations into the therapy setting to be analyzed and discussed.

 This app should be utilized only in conjunction with a speech-language pathologist who specializes is dysfluency. Stuttering can become worse if not managed properly.

i-SPEAK

by SDC

www.defstut.com/Ispeak.html

$9.99

↘ FROM THE DEVELOPER

DAF stands for "delayed auditory feedback." When you use *i-Speak*, the signal of the stammerer's voice will be played back to him or her more slowly, at speeds that you can choose. The range is from 20 to 300 ms (milliseconds). FAF stands for "frequency altered feedback." When you use the application, the signal of the stammerer's voice will be pitched to a higher or lower frequency, which you can customize.

↘ CUSTOMER REVIEW

i-Speak is a fantastic tool for fluency shaping, especially when used with headphones or a Bluetooth. Fluency can increase from 70%-90% instantly and with the guidance of a speech pathologist, good speech habits can be maintained.

 It is strongly recommended that *i-Speak*, and any other app/device that focuses on dysfluency, be used in conjunction with a licensed speech pathologist who specializes in dysfluency.

DAF ASSISTANT

by ARTEFACT, LLC

http://artefactsoft.com/iphonedaf.htm

$9.99

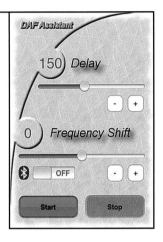

↘ FROM THE DEVELOPER

DAF Assistant implements Delayed Auditory Feedback (DAF) and Frequency-shifting Auditory Feedback (FAF) techniques that are known to help people with stuttering to speak more fluently.

↘ CUSTOMER REVIEW

DAF Assistant works best with headsets or a Bluetooth. Individuals with dysfluency will not stand out as different when using an app in conjunction with an iDevice to help remediate stuttering. I urge anyone considering the use of DAF or FAF to research the apps and obtain the advice of a licensed speech pathologist.

 It is highly recommended that *DAF Assistant* or any other app/device that focuses on dysfluency be used under the guidance of a licensed speech pathologist who specializes in stuttering and dysfluency.

DISFLUENCY INDEX COUNTER

by Smarty Ears

www.smarty-ears.com

$9.99

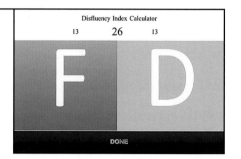

↘ FROM THE DEVELOPER

The *Disfluency Index Counter* app allows speech and language therapists to perform a live count of the number of fluent or disfluent syllables. It saves you time and makes figuring out the percentage of stuttered syllables a lot easier—we do it for you!

↘ CUSTOMER REVIEW

Disfluency Index Counter is a straightforward app that tracks and calculates data for the user (speech pathologist). Any app that takes my data, crunches it, and then emails it to me is worth its weight in gold.

Part X

Creative Learning

Music has an innate effect on all individuals to induce positive self-expression both verbal and nonverbal. Creative parents, caregivers, and teachers have been using music and song to teach language, concepts, encourage participation in daily activities, calm nerves, and reinforce students of all ages. Music and song are effective because they are naturally reinforcing, immediate in time, and provide motivation for practicing non-musical skills. Most importantly, music is successful because everyone responds positively to some type of tune.

Many iDevices are made for music and iTunes offers thousands of selections from classical and opera to "Old MacDonald" and from Punk Rock to Pop. Students who may otherwise refuse to wear headphones or ear buds will put them on to listen to music. Here is a chance to use an iDevice as the world does—listening to music. Additionally, make some music of your own!

Chapter 29:
Music, Song & Creativity

The American Music Therapy Association affirms that music is a stimulus to achieve non-musical treatment goals. Music is used to promote learning and skill acquisition with students on the spectrum and in special education. There is evidence-based research to support the connection between music (singing-rhythm) and the development of language, speech, creativity, movement, memory for songs and memory for academic material. Overall, music enhances mood, attention, flexibility, behavior and optimizes the student's ability to learn. Hans Christian Anderson expressed it best with, "When words fail, music speaks."

Success Story: Fiona

Fiona is a tiny six-year-old whirlwind. Her first day of school was exhausting for her and the staff. She could not stop moving, climbing, and squirming. By lunchtime she was so tired and hungry, she began crying and pulling her hair, nevertheless, she kept moving. Her teacher noticed that he may have heard her hum the tune to "Wheels on the Bus." I quickly opened the Wheels on the Bus app and turned the volume up. When she heard the music, she stopped crying and pulling her hair. Fiona sat next to me for the next half hour exploring the app. She was then able to eat her lunch and make it through the rest of the day. Her teacher now has Wheels on the Bus on his iPhone. Day Saved!

WHEELS ON THE BUS

by Duck Duck Moose

http://duckduckmoosedesign.com

$0.99

FROM THE DEVELOPER

Created by parents, *Wheels on the Bus* is a fun, interactive musical book, based on the popular children's song. Come aboard the bus to spin the wheels, open and close the doors, swish the wipers, pop some bubbles, make a dog bark, and much more! Delight your children while encouraging cognitive, language, and motor development.

CUSTOMER REVIEW

Wheels on the Bus is very popular with all my younger students. Take the time to make your own recording of the song as the original is too fast—any student with auditory processing difficulties will have a hard time differentiating among the words. Students like the ability to change languages and instruments. *Wheels on the Bus* is also a book, the sound can be turned off, and it is a fun, interactive reading activity.

OLD MACDONALD

by Duck Duck Moose

http://duckduckmoosedesign.com

$1.99

FROM THE DEVELOPER

Old MacDonald is a musical book with 12 colorful pages of fully interactive, original illustrations. Visit this farm where you can shear a sheep, push a tractor, flip a cow, make a chicken cluck, see pigs scurry, and watch ducks waddle. This unique rendition of the classic song also includes many new surprises: a philosopher cow, the painter Pig-casso, disco dancing sheep, mid-century modern furniture, spaceships, floating balloons, a bulldozer, a dump truck, and much more!

CUSTOMER REVIEW

Old MacDonald would be a great interactive book; however, there is only one written word per page. Change the language or the instrument for more variety. *Old MacDonald* can actually help you learn a foreign language as there are five languages available on this app. It can be used as a reinforcer or learning activity.

ITSY BITSY SPIDER

by Duck Duck Moose

http://duckduckmoosedesign.com

$0.99

FROM THE DEVELOPER

Itsy Bitsy Spider is based on a popular song, but this new app is even more interactive and has more educational activities to engage children. The app is like an interactive movie, panning to a different scene each time you poke the spider. A friendly tutor (a fly!) teaches your child about nature and the environment.

CUSTOMER REVIEW

Itsy Bitsy Spider is very interactive; however, there are no written words. If a student has difficulty with auditory processing, you can make your own recording as the soundtrack may be difficult to understand. Touching the spider changes the page (pretty cute). *Itsy Bitsy Spider* has counting, fun facts, a hat game, and collecting eggs embedded into the app.

KIDS VIDEOS AND ENTERTAINMENT – KIDEOS HD

by Big Purple Hippos

www.kideos.com

$2.99 (iPhone) or $3.99 (iPad)

FROM THE DEVELOPER

The *Kideos* iPhone app allows children to safely watch their favorite videos on the go. *Kideos* is simple for children to use on their own and every video has been reviewed by a select group of parents and educators.

CUSTOMER REVIEW

I can let my children watch videos from the Internet with no worries! *Kideos* plays all the most popular, kid-friendly, Video Advisory Council-approved online videos and games with regular updates. Videos are divided into age appropriateness, channels, and custom playlists. A search bar lets the user find special interest topics. Most videos have educational value; however, some are just plain fun. This is a highly recommended app for education, reinforcement, and filling downtime. Check out "Our Story" in the "About" section of the *Kideos* website for a warmhearted developer's story.

PANDORA RADIO

by Pandora Media, Inc.

www.pandora.com/#/

FREE

FROM THE DEVELOPER

Pandora Radio is your own free personalized radio station, now available to stream music on your iPhone or iPad. Just start with the name of one of your favorite artists, songs, or classical composers and Pandora will create a "station" that plays your music and more music like it.

CUSTOMER REVIEW

Pandora Radio lets users create a radio station as diverse as they are. Tell *Pandora Radio* the names of your favorite songs and musicians, then Pandora will create a radio station that will play those songs and similar songs. It's free!

MAGIC PIANO

by Smule

http://magicpiano.smule.com

$0.99

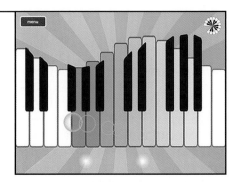

FROM THE DEVELOPER

Play timeless pieces on spiral and circular keyboards, or follow beams of light—mastery requires only imagination. Play alone, or travel through a warp hole and play Piano Roulette with other performers across the world.

CUSTOMER REVIEW

Magic Piano is one of my all time favorite apps! I have prevented meltdowns with this app because it is so desirable. *Magic Piano* can be simple or complicated, depending on the level of the student. It is visually beautiful in all modes. Occupational therapists love this app: *Magic Piano* combines sensory, motor coordination, eye-hand coordination, and finger isolation goals into one activity. Best of all, the students don't know they are working. Beautiful, therapeutic, and artistic, everyone should have *Magic Piano* on their iDevice.

FACES iMAKE

by iMagine machine LLC

www.imaginemachine.com

$1.99

FROM THE DEVELOPER

Faces iMake is all about stimulating the right brain and giving kids a fun and playful educational environment. The app encourages kids to solve problems creatively, to innovate, to see things from a different perspective, and to create obvious forms with the most unexpected combination of objects.

CUSTOMER REVIEW

Faces iMake spurs creativity, encourages pretending, and a bit of the sillies. This is the most fun you can have while labeling, describing, categorizing, and targeting fine motor skills. Show off your creations via email or your social network. *Faces iMake* comes with catchy music or you can choose your own music selection from your music library. iMagine offers a free version of *Faces iMake*, so give it a try.

FINGERPIANO

by Junpei Wada

http://fingerpiano.net/fingerpiano

$1.99 (iPhone) or $2.99 (iPad)

FROM THE DEVELOPER

FingerPiano allows you to play the piano with just your finger. You don't need any skill, scores, or practice; you only need the motivation to play music. Instead of reading the score, scrolling guides appear on the screen—Just touch the keyboard to create beautiful music!

CUSTOMER REVIEW

Get this app! *FingerPiano* can be utilized for occupational therapy, serve as a reinforcer, build self esteem, or to follow visual directions. A young student of mine at the single word level uttered his first sentence to gain access to *FingerPiano*. Another prompt-dependant student independently uses all features of *FingerPiano*. Some students will put on performances, others will sit and play for as long as I let them. The uses are endless. Developers, please add contemporary music! Try the free version to see if *FingerPiano* is the right app for you.

TAPPYTUNES™

by UtiliTouch, Inc.

http://utilitouch.com/tappytunes

$1.99

FROM THE DEVELOPER

Play your favorite tunes instantly and note-perfectly just by tapping!

CUSTOMER REVIEW

Anyone, really anyone, can play a tune on *TappyTunes*. Turn your iPad into an instrument with 80 songs, each with animated graphics and sound effects that fit the theme of the song. All the notes of the songs are pre-recorded, so all the user has to do is tap the screen to the beat and hear the music. *TappyTunes* supplies the music and you supply the lyrics. *TappyTunes* can be used to build focus and attention, motor skills, turn-taking, self-esteem, or as an effective rienforcer. Try the free version, *TappyTunes* Lite, and you will be leading sing-alongs in no time.

DRUM KIT

by CrimsonJet, Inc.

http://crimsonjet.com

$0.99

FROM THE DEVELOPER

Ever wanted to play the drums? This is the closest you can get without a real kit. This is a fun app for drummers and non-drummers alike. Impress your friends with your chops, or play along to songs from your iPod music library.

CUSTOMER REVIEW

Drum Kit is a motivating way to encourage students to participate in motor coordination activities. The sound is fair, but the look is real. Try the free version and take a look at the videos on You Tube before purchasing this app. I have eyewitness accounts of occupational therapists using this app successfully for finger isolation tasks.

BABY PIANO

by Dream Cortex

www.dreamcortex.com

$1.99

FROM THE DEVELOPER

Baby Piano offers great fun that keeps your kids amused while learning to enjoy and explore music. The colorful interface and cute animal icons are eye-catching to kids, thus stimulating their interest in playing music.

CUSTOMER REVIEW

Baby Piano acts as a therapy tool and a reinforcer in one app. I use it for color, animal, and letter identification. Occupational therapists use it for motor control, finger isolation, and eye-hand coordination. The students just think it's fun. *Baby Piano* has eight keys and plays eight songs. Students can play a song by touching the notes or go freestyle. The best part is, the animals can also make music. Switch from piano to animal sounds.

 The record and playback feature is five seconds long. This can be frustrating. Try the free version and let your students decide.

FUN PIANO

by Gravity

website currently unavailable

$1.99

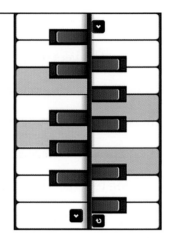

FROM THE DEVELOPER

Play *Fun Piano* with your friends! Rotate the keyboard and you can teach someone to play the piano. Enjoy!

CUSTOMER REVIEW

I like the *Fun Piano* app because it is interactive: I can play with a student. The student and I can take turns being the leader to create a tune. When the leader presses a key, the corresponding key (on the other side of the pad) will turn blue.

Part XI

Information for Parents & Caregivers

Remember the words of Temple Grandin's mother who explains that autism makes Temple "different" but not "less." When a child is diagnosed with autism or a disability, caregivers often feel a range of emotions as well as feeling overwhelmed. Obtaining accurate information regarding their child's disability and the resources that are available is a first step. Doctors, healthcare professionals, educators, and support groups can all be invaluable resources in determining what combination of interventions and services are right for your child. The World Wide Web provides a virtual plethora of information for individuals with disabilities, as do the following apps.

Chapter 30: Information about Autism

"Knowledge is power (Ipsa Scientia Potestas Est)."

—Sir Francis Bacon

NO MORE MELTDOWNS

by SymTrend, Inc.

www.symtrend.com/tw/nmm-public

$10.99

FROM THE DEVELOPER

It could happen at home, school, the grocery store, or a restaurant. Meltdowns are stressful for both child and adult, but Dr. Baker's *No More Meltdowns* app can help!

CUSTOMER REVIEW

No More Meltdowns provides caregivers basic techniques for preventing, and if necessary, managing meltdowns. Give your child and yourself the tools needed to deal with challenging situations and the ability to analyze triggers. *No More Meltdowns* comes with a companion website that allows the user keep an "electronic diary" that tracks, analyzes data, and identifies situations that may be a challenge to your child. *No More Meltdowns* offers the user lots of basic information on managing feelings, identifying triggers, and preventative strategies.

 No More Meltdowns can track data on one child. For a comprehensive resource on preventing and managing meltdowns, please refer to Dr. Baker's book, *No More Meltdowns*.

TEMPLE GRANDIN

by Autism Research Institute

www.templegrandin.com

FREE

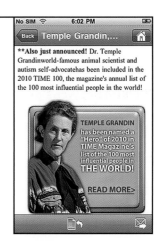

FROM THE DEVELOPER

This free application retrieves information such as Dr. Grandin's articles, speaking appearances, and information on how to order her books from her website, www.TempleGrandin.com, and presents it in an easy-to-read format.

CUSTOMER REVIEW

Keep up with one of the most influential people in the world by adding the *Temple Grandin* app to your iDevice. Do you want to know where her next conference will be? Are you interested in learning more about autism, searching for information on humane livestock handling, or just want to join Temple's mailing list? All the information on Temple Grandin's website is now also available in app format.

AUTISM NEWS READER

by Splaysoft, LLC

www.splaysoft.com

$0.99

FROM THE DEVELOPER

The *Autism News Reader* grabs the top stories from the best autism health news and information sites and delivers them to your iPhone, iPad or iPod touch. Keep up with autism issues and developments in one place—*Autism News Reader*. You can add your own news feeds, view in Landscape mode, and share stories with friends and family.

CUSTOMER REVIEW

I no longer have to spend hours sorting through articles, newsletters, and emails for up-to-date reliable information. I can easily find the latest scientific, human interest, and educational/conference information as well as instant access to websites, blogs, and discussions. This *Autism News Reader* is a huge time saver.

AUTISMTRACK

by Handhold Adaptive, LLC

www.handholdadaptive.com

$49.99

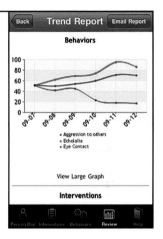

FROM THE DEVELOPER

AutismTrack features daily log screens that provide a snapshot of any particular day's interventions and behaviors. Users may also graph symptoms and monitor compliance over periods of time. These daily logs and trend reports may be emailed (in PDF format), so that parents and other caregivers can review useful information on their search to discover the unique patterns and trends experienced by individuals with autism spectrum disorders (ASD).

CUSTOMER REVIEW

Track your child's behaviors and analyze trends to design custom interventions that work for individual needs. *AutismTrack* monitors five behaviors and nine interventions to allow caregivers and educators to determine which treatment options are right for each student or child. Additional interventions and behaviors can be added for enhanced customization. Parents and educators can enter data and add notes to encourage teamwork and carryover throughout the day. Once interventions, behaviors, and trends have been reviewed the user can email the data to each member of the team or make a printout to keep for records.

AUTISMTEST

by Paws4Roel

www.paws4roel.com

FREE

FROM THE DEVELOPER

Have you ever wondered if you, your child, or someone you know is on the autism spectrum? Although not a diagnostic tool, it is accurate and can certainly be used as a guideline. Contacting a professional for further information is highly recommended, however.

CUSTOMER REVIEW

The *AutismTest* app should be used for information only. This app does not diagnose! There have been false positives and negatives. If you are concerned about yourself or another, please see a specialist. When seeking a specialist, please make sure that person is familiar with autism spectrum disorder. That being said, this is a place to start if you are wondering if you should get yourself or your child screened. There are 50 multiple choice questions to answer: agree, slightly agree, disagree, and slightly disagree. There are 37 yes/no questions for the child test. I scored slightly autistic.

 If you accidentally touch the wrong part of the screen, you have to start over again. I had to do this twice. *AutismTest* has some good resources and information regarding autism. Donations are solicited at the end of the test.

AUTISM M-CHAT TODDLER SCREENING TOOL

by iCrysta

http://icrysta.com

$3.99

FROM THE DEVELOPER

Are you a pediatrician, a physician, or NP that works with young children? Are you giving the *Autism M-CHAT* to your patients? This validated tool is reimbursable to you by insurance providers. The *M-CHAT* can be taken directly on the iPod, iPad or iPhone and it is very easy to use! Scoring is instant. After Part One is complete, the app will tell you if you need to proceed with Part Two of the screening.

CUSTOMER REVIEW

Autism M-CHAT Toddler Screening Tool should be used for information in conjunction with a physician. The Modified Checklist for Autism in Toddlers (*M-CHAT*) is used to access the risk of autism in toddlers between 16 and 30 months. It is also designed to bring awareness to those who use it. *M-CHAT* has two parts: a checklist and a follow-up interview. Please see a specialist for diagnostic purposes.

IEP CHECKLIST

by Nurvee

www.peatc.org

FREE

FROM THE DEVELOPER

The *IEP Checklist* is a tool for parents and teachers to consider as they develop the IEP. Not every item on the checklist is required by special education regulations. For more information, consult the Federal regulations and other information that can be found at http://idea.ed.gov.

CUSTOMER REVIEW

Special education laws can be lengthy, vague, and misinterpreted by any member of the IEP team. *IEP Checklist* offers a quick reference to the laws and can be accessed at a moment's notice and, if necessary, in the IEP itself. Parents, teachers, and professionals alike find the task of understanding all the special education laws daunting and often confusing. Every school district will have a distinct interpretation of the laws and conduct IEP meetings according to their understanding of the guidelines. The *IEP Checklist* serves as a reminder to participants of what is legally required from an IEP.

Chapter 31: Gluten Free

A gluten-free diet simply means avoiding foods or drinks that contain gluten (wheat, barley, rye, oats, or anything made from these grains). Some suggest that individuals with autism have gastrointestinal difficulties that make it hard to digest grains properly, affecting behavior adversely. Maintaining a gluten-free diet is difficult because gluten is present in many foods and can be hidden in prepared foods. Let's take some of the workload off parents, caregivers, and individuals by providing this information at their fingertips.

IS THAT GLUTEN FREE?

by Midlife Crisis Apps, LLC

www.midlifecrisisapps.com/Midlife_Crisis_Apps/Is_That_Gluten_Free.html

$7.99

FROM THE DEVELOPER

Is That Gluten Free? is designed for those with gluten sensitivities, Celiac Disease, or anyone wanting more information on gluten-free products or leading a gluten-free lifestyle.

CUSTOMER REVIEW

The *Is That Gluten Free?* app has compiled tons of information to answer the question, "Is that gluten free?" The "Defeat Autism Now! Protocol" recommends that every child with autism be placed on a gluten-free, casein-free diet for at least three months. *Is That Gluten Free?* can help caregivers and individuals with this seemingly overwhelming task of identifying food products that are truly gluten-free. I know from personal experience that diet can make a difference.

 Please do not try any diet without the guidance of a physician and/or nutritionist. Every person is different; not every individual on the spectrum will benefit from a gluten-free diet.

ICANEAT ONTHEGO GLUTEN & ALLERGEN FREE

by AllergyFree Passport

http://allergyfreepassport.com/mobile-apps/icaneat-onthego

$2.99

FROM THE DEVELOPER

Personalize fast food menus by identifying nine common food allergens in meal options from 20 restaurant chains, with 14 chains addressing gluten. No Internet connectivity is required to access more than 2,100 menu items with free updates provided! View only items you can eat by hiding those containing your allergens.

CUSTOMER REVIEW

iCanEat OnTheGo Gluten & Allergen Free provides individuals and caregivers easy access to invaluable dietary information for 20 fast food menus. Recent literature has suggested that food allergies play a role in causing or worsening autism. While this has not been proven, many parents have noted positive changes in behavior when certain foods have been removed from their child's diet.

 We all know that every individual, as well as his or her diet and possible food sensitivities, is different. Consult a physician and/or nutritionist prior to starting any diet.

Part XII

Cool Stuff

Now that we have equipped individuals with disabilities with the tools more befitting to who they are—COOL—let's take it a step further: SUPER COOL! In this chapter, I will take it over the top with gadgets, cases, holders, and yes, even clothing. Some of the items in this chapter are beneficial, some are protective, some crucial, and others are completely outrageous!

Chapter 32: Cool Stuff

Just as there is a flurry of activity by developers creating apps, there is a flurry of activity by manufactures creating accessories to make your iDevices easier to access, better grip, great protection, and enhance the utility. This chapter gives examples of covers, cases, stands, audio equipment, clothing, and other useful accessories to increase the usability of your iDevice.

From building language in the backseat to keeping your hands warm on a winter day you can choose your color and style to best fit your personality. Whether you are a minimalist or like to show your style, there is an accessory for that.

iADAPTER

by AMDi

www.amdi.net/iadapter

$198.00

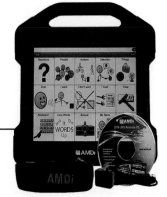

FROM THE DEVELOPER

Protect your iPad from damage with our all new iAdapter™ housing, complete with rubberized corners and handle. A small slide cover on the front of the housing will hide the home button from roaming fingers that will close running applications. The iAdapter is also an amplifier with dual speakers that will deliver clean, crisp sound that can be heard in the noisiest of settings. It comes with a rechargeable, lithium-polymer battery, shoulder strap for portability, and a plastic stand for table top use.

CUSTOMER REVIEW

Wow! iAdapter offers the user all the great features we have been asking for: durability, speakers, a wheelchair mount, and a way to block curious fingers from pressing that pesky little "home" button. Please visit the website for more information and additional accessories. With iAdapter, the iPad is now just as durable as any other device on the market.

OTTERBOX DEFENDER SERIES FOR APPLE®

by OtterBox

www.otterbox.com

iPad: $89.95

iPhone: $49.95

iPod touch: $29.95

FROM THE DEVELOPER

Drop-proof your magical, new, must-have gadgets with the OtterBox Defender Series for Apple devices! This cutting-edge case incorporates three layers of hardcore protection plus some advanced features.

CUSTOMER REVIEW

The OtterBox Defender protects against everything except spills (liquid). It provides three layers of dust-, bump-, and drop-protection while allowing complete access to all functions. Defender cases are highly recommended for individuals who may drop or bump their iDevice or have others in their environment who may do the same.

iMAINGO 2 & iMAINGO X

by Portable Sound Laboratories, Inc.

www.imaingo.com

$39.95 (iMainGo 2)

$69.95 (iMainGo X)

iMainGo 2 goes wherever you do—there's no need to

plug it in or recharge. Its advanced design gives its four AAA batteries (included) unprecedented life—up to 30 hours. iMainGo X comes with a rechargeable lithium-ion battery, two headphone jacks, external power controls, daisy-chain feature, custom travel bag, and extra carry strap.

CUSTOMER REVIEW

I have had great success with the iMainGo speakers. Teachers have borrowed the iMainGo system to boost audio for an entire classroom. Protect your iPod touch or iPhone from bumps and drops with iMainGo's sturdy edifice.

 iMainGo has a plastic cover over the face of the iDevice. This cover could make it more challenging for some individuals to access the touch screen.

LIVESPEAKR

by Digital Group Audio (DGA)

www.livespeakr.com

$69.99

FROM THE DEVELOPER

Livespeakr is the ultra-portable and multifunctional speaker system that gives you the power of a dock in the palm of your hand!

CUSTOMER REVIEW

Is your iPod touch or iPhone simply not loud enough? Try Livespeakr. The cradle can rotate your iPod touch in both portrait and landscape modes. Livespeakr is small enough to fit into a pocket, purse, or backpack. The built-in rechargeable battery can last up to 16 hours. There is not a protective covering around your iPod touch. This allows complete access to all controls; however, it may also leave it open to damage. For more information, take a look at the product overview video on the website.

Waterproof your iDevice

ZIPLOC BAGS

CUSTOMER REVIEW

Waterproof and spill-proof your wonderful iDevices with a simple plastic bag. You can put your iDevices into a Ziploc plastic bag and still use the touch screen. I use the Ziplocs during snacks and mealtime to prevent damage from sticky, wet spills. The plastic bags work excellently in this capacity. Use the Ziplocs anytime the environment may be clammy, damp, or soggy such as rainy days, in the shower room, or cooking dinner.

Obviously the plastic bag has its limits. Do not take into the swimming pool or submerge it underwater or your iDevice could drown. For extra protection use freezer bags.

iPAD MOUNTS

by RJ Cooper & Associates, Inc.

www.rjcooper.com/tablet-mounts/index.html

Prices vary according to needs

FROM THE DEVELOPER

Hi! I'm R.J. Cooper and I make special software and hardware products for persons with special needs.

CUSTOMER REVIEW

For iDevice mounts, clamps, stands, and bumper cases this is your place. RJ offers two sizes of "arms" that are positionable and secure. Both "arms" include clamps that can attach to tables, desks, and bedrails. See RJ's website for more information, prices and pictures. iPad Mounts are also great for lightweight AAC devices and Netbooks!

THE iPAD CORDLESS SUPER-SWITCH

by RJ Cooper & Associates, Inc.

www.rjcooper.com/super-switch/index.html

$149.00

FROM THE DEVELOPER

This one switch does it all! Its 5" diameter makes a great target for those who need it. And its built-in switch interface can work with any switch for "Auto" or "Step" scanning. The iPad Cordless Super-Switch works through Bluetooth 2.1 for simple pairing and range of over 50 feet. Any app that has been pro-grammed for switch access can use my iPad Super Switch. Most AAC app developers are incorporating switch access, which will work with my devices. It has a lithium-ion battery that recharges through your USB port or USB AC charger.

CUSTOMER REVIEW

Thanks, RJ Cooper, for exploring the use of switches with iDevices. I hope the developers will provide scanning options on all apps.

 Currently, not all apps will work with switches.

THE iPAD CORDLESS SWITCH INTERFACE

by RJ Cooper & Associates, Inc.

www.rjcooper.com/cordless-switch-interface/index.html

$99.00

FROM THE DEVELOPER

That's right. Switch access to iPads! Plug any switch into it for cause/effect, switch timing practice, AAC auto-scan and step-scan, spelling, and any other apps on the horizon! The iPad Cordless Switch Interface works through Bluetooth 2.1 for simple pairing and range of over 50 feet. Any app that has been programmed for switch access can use my iPad Cordless Switch Interface. Most AAC app developers are incorporating switch access, which will work with my devices. It has a lithium-ion battery that recharges through your USB port or USB AC charger.

ETRE TOUCHY GLOVES & FIVEPOINT GLOVES

by Etre Touchy

www.etretouchy.com/buy

Etre Touchy Gloves: £19.99 (about $30.40/€24.22)

FIVEPOINT Gloves: £24.99 (about $39.53/€29.85)

FROM THE DEVELOPER

Etre Touchy Gloves are a stylish, fun, and practical way to keep your hands warm while using your touch screen phone, portable games system, media player, and other electronic gadgets. Their missing thumb and index fingertips give you the freedom to touch, tap, stroke, slide, and pinch your iDevice's controls in any way you desire. FIVEPOINT Gloves are a stylish way of keeping your hands warm and dry while using your iPhone, iPad, iPod, and other touch-screen devices. Thanks to their specially-designed conductive fingertips, they do what other gloves don't: they let you touch, tap, and type on touch-screens without having to take them off.

CUSTOMER REVIEW

How nice are these! Etre Touchy Gloves come in a selection of great stylish colors, or if you are ordering for a group (20+), you can select from 120 different shades. Imagine keeping your hands warm and cozy while operating your device in the cold winter months. Etre Touchy Gloves are 100% pure wool; launder with care. Wash in cold water and air dry.

 Etre Touchy is located in London; however, they will ship anywhere.

UNIVERSAL GAME WHEEL & PARABOLIC SOUND SPHERE

by Allsop

www.clingo.com

(Universal Game Wheel) $19.99

(Parabolic Sound Sphere) $34.99

FROM THE DEVELOPER

It's pretty simple, really. Clingo products hold your phone. It doesn't matter if it is a BlackBerry, iPhone, Droid, Samsung, or whatever. Whether in your car, at the office, at home, or wherever, Clingo holds it. Any phone, anywhere.

CUSTOMER REVIEW

I found Clingo last year at MacWorld. The vendor gave it to me for a free trial. I was a little skeptical, at first, about the Gel Pad. My students not only love the gaming/sporty look of the Universal Game Wheel, they can actually hold an iPod touch with ease. As for the Gel Pad, it still sticks! One year later, and many, many hands, the Gel Pad has never released my iPod touch and the students have never dropped the Game Wheel. I have cleaned it twice, following manufacturer's directions with no problems. The Parabolic Sound Sphere is also a great product that enhances the audio without speakers. Again, my students have had no problems holding the Sphere. Take a look at all Clingo products to find the one that fits your needs.

iTEE & iDRESS

by iClothing

www.iclothing.com.au

iTee: $39.95

iDress: $89.95

FROM THE DEVELOPER

Need an easy way to carry your iPad? iClothing provides
an easy, comfortable way to store your iPad on the go.
Original iTee and iDress feature reinforced padded pouches
that are comfortable and almost invisible.

CUSTOMER REVIEW

Where did I put that iPad? With iClothing, your iPad will always be conveniently available. iClothing is an ingenious method of keeping your iDevice close at hand and out
of harm's way at all times. Recommended for parents, caregivers, educators, individuals
with disabilities, and of course, fashion-conscious individuals on their way to Starbucks.
The iDress comes in black, while the iTees come in black or white. I am going to order the
little black iDress for dinner parties; size 8 please.

 Remove iPad before washing!

iPAD HEADREST MOUNT

by BoxWave

www.boxwave.com/products/headrestmount/
apple-iPad-headrest-mount_3779.htm

$44.95

FROM THE DEVELOPER

BoxWave's Headrest Mount is not only a case, but an all-in-one mounting solution that gives your car passengers hands-free viewing of your Apple iPad. Perfect for those long trips, the Headrest Mount will keep your kids entertained and occupied so that you can focus and enjoy the ride!

CUSTOMER REVIEW

iPad Headrest Mount offers on-the-go communication, education, and entertainment for those in the back seat. Just button your iPad into the Headrest Mount and you will not have to worry about spills, drops, or crushing your iPad with packages. Your iPad is accessible and safe on the road.

MINI CAPACITIVE STYLUS

by BoxWave

www.boxwave.com/products/
minicapacitivestylus/index.htm

$14.95

FROM THE DEVELOPER

The mini Capacitive Stylus enables you to use your device without ever touching the screen with your finger! Its portable size makes it easy to carry around, and can be stored away by attaching to your iDevice's 3.5 mm headphone jack.

CUSTOMER REVIEW

Unable to access your touch screen with the pads of your fingers? Try a stylus. The mini Capacitive Stylus can fit easily into a pocket or attach to your iDevice via the headphone jack.

UNIVERSAL CAPACITIVE STYLUS

by BoxWave

www.boxwave.com/products/
universalcapacitivestylusindex.htm

$20.95

FROM THE DEVELOPER

BoxWave's Universal Capacitive Stylus allows you to use your iDevice without ever touching the screen with your finger.

CUSTOMER REVIEW

If you have long fingernails, wear gloves, or have difficulty accessing your iDevice's touch screen capabilities, try a stylus. The Universal Capacitive Stylus works on all touch screens and is stylish and durable.

ePILLOW

by Veyl Products, LLC

www.epillow.net

$19.95

FROM THE DEVELOPER

Use your iPad comfortably anywhere, anytime, even sitting in bed or on the couch. With ePillow™, you won't get tired of holding your iPad and it's perfect for watching movies with a friend.

CUSTOMER REVIEW

For those individuals who are bedbound, chair bound, or have orthopedic challenges, ePillow is a handy solution for making your iPad more obtainable. The adjustable viewing angle gives the user the choice of landscape or portrait modes. ePillow can be used with most protective cases. Take a look at the short video provided on the website for more information. ePillow is 18" x 11" and comes in black and brown.

CHILL PILL AUDIO RAPCAP MICROPHONE

by Chill Pill Audio

www.handhelditems.com/chill-pill-audio-rapcap-microphone-p-115487.html

$14.99

FROM THE DEVELOPER

Chill Pill Audio RapCap's high-quality microphone captures crisp, clear audio and is optimized for voice recordings. Just plug it into your iPod or iPhone's headphone port and you're ready to go. You can listen to your recordings immediately after you capture them or transfer them to your computer using iTunes.

CUSTOMER REVIEW

Now you can personalize all those wonderful customizable apps on your iPod touch. Chill Pill Audio RapCap Microphone is small and portable. Its unobtrusive style makes it the perfect microphone for capturing audio on the go.

 RapCap's size (about that of a gumdrop) makes it a choking hazard. If your child or student tends to put inappropriate objects into their mouth, then RapCap may not be your best choice.

ELITE HOME THEATER SEATING

by Elite Home Theater Seating

www.elitehometheaterseating.com/iPad-chair.html

Starts at $2,495.00

FROM THE DEVELOPER

Elite Home Theater Seating offers an ergonomically designed chair specifically custom tailored for optimum iPad use.

CUSTOMER REVIEW

Oh Yeah! Check them out on YouTube: http://www.youtube.com/watch?v=hog9cijGOEM& feature=player_embedded.

iPAD SUIT

by Mohan's Custom Tailors

www.mohantailors.com

$600.00

CUSTOMER REVIEW

An upscale Manhattan tailor has designed a $600 suit jacket with an iPad pocket. Mohan's custom tailors, founded in the '70s before men needed gadget pockets, said the somewhat gimmicky-looking iPad suit is the result of customer requests. This one falls into the "REALLY?" category.

iCARTA STEREO DOCK FOR iPOD® WITH BATH TISSUE HOLDER

by Atech Flash Technology

www.atechflash.com

$29.99 (after $10.00 rebate)

FROM THE DEVELOPER

Now you can enhance your experience in any room with your favorite music from your iPod.

CUSTOMER REVIEW

Don't laugh, iCarta Stereo Dock for iPod with Bath Tissue Holder is an invaluable tool when it comes to encouraging daily hygiene routines, especially toileting. Plenty of parents have bought an iDevice just for the purpose of potty training. It is highly motivating and can provide visual and audio supports as well as reinforcement.

 iCarta requires AC Power (AC Adapter included) and has limited ability to charge. It will not charge iPhone 3G/3GS, iPod touch 2G and up, iPod Nano 4G and up.

Conclusion

Bear in mind, there are over 425,000 apps available with more added to the list every day. I have made an attempt to provide you with an excellent list of potentially invaluable apps to support individuals with disabilities in their daily lives; however, there are jillions more. It is my sincere hope that I have provided enough information for you to use your iDevices to their fullest capacities and individualize your app selection to fit your personal needs. Remember, even though technology is moving forward at a rapid pace, your iDevice will last for years. The apps, movies, and music you put on your iDevices today will continually be updated—usually for free—and remain relevant. If not, simply change the content as your needs and goals change. I have the first iPod that Apple put on the market. The iPod is still working; however, I have changed its content several times. Your iDevice will last a long time.

If this book has assisted you with communication, educational, social, leisure activities, and aspirations, I'd love to hear from you. Contact me at www.proactivespeechtherapy.com and loisjeanbrady@gmail.com, or catch me on Facebook. (Search: Lois Jean Brady.)

Giving Something Back:
The iDevice Recycle Program _____

Portable, socially cool devices like the iPad, iPod touch and iPhone are invaluable for communication, education, social, and leisure skills. Not to mention that they are inexpensive and fun to use. However, not every individual who could benefit from an iDevice has access to one. I am so excited about the possibilities of this new technology that I would like to see that every individual who could benefit from an iDevice (educators, individuals, parents, and caregivers) has access to one. To that end, I am asking for donations of working iDevices. I will furnish the iDevices with apps and offer them to individuals who would not otherwise have access to these wonderful Apple creations.

Let's put an iPad, iPod touch or iPhone into the hands of every individual who would benefit from them!

Please send your iDevices to:

> Apps for Autism
>
> 649 Main St., #229
>
> Martinez, CA 94553

Keep Updated on All the Latest, Greatest Info

There has been a tremendous explosion of technology, which has become a crucial element in the lives of individuals with disabilities. The problem, however, is finding an effortless, dependable way to keep up with the ebb and flow of the latest technology.

So how do you do it? How do you keep up with technology and still have time in the day for your job, your family, and yourself? Below are two practical resources that will keep you updated with the latest trends, news, apps, developers, and updates without having to spend countless hours searching the Internet or combing through articles and blogs.

Future Horizons—www.FHautism.com

Future Horizons has a great companion website for this book! A place where readers or anyone can come to learn about iTherapy, download app updates, get the latest information on new apps, blog about their experiences, and join an online community to support and learn about the best technology has to offer individuals with disabilities.

Autism Hangout—www.autismhangout.com

The Autism Hangout is one of my favorite places to find information, discussions, and insights on how best to thrive with autism. Ironically, the Autism Hangout offers a Feature Program Series called "Apps for Autism." Apps for Autism is an ongoing, continually updated series that provides information on what's new, helpful, and hopeful in the world of technology, enhanced with insightful interviews with the developers themselves. All Feature Programs are linked to Discussion Forums for further discussion, sharing, and insights with others.

References

References

There is no doubt that Steve Jobs and Apple are in the forefront when it comes to personal-use computing technology. Apple revolutionized the way we communicate, carry out business, read a book, and even watch a movie.

Even if it wasn't intentional, the fact still remains: Apple's line of products directly impacts the growing needs of those with autism and other special needs. Interesting and groundbreaking uses of Apple technology is on the rise, fueled by the growing number of Apps and the growing number of teachers, therapists, and clinicians using the technology.

Although still in its infancy, there is some research and a myriad of blogs, articles, and websites available on the Internet that cover topics like how to choose specific apps and use the technology (an iDevice) in way that is relevant, meaningful, and evidence-based.

Below is a short list of recommended readings and research that support using iDevices with your population.

American Academy of Pediatrics Council on Communications and Media. (2010). Policy Statement - Media Education. *Pediatrics*, 126(5), 1-6. Doi: 10.1542/peds.2010-1636.

Apple Education. (2006). iPod helps special-needs students make the grade. *Apple Education*. Retrieved October 12, 2006, from www.apple.com/education/profiles/louisamuscatine.

ASHA. (2011). *Applications (apps) for speech-language pathology practice*. Retrieved from www.asha.org/SLP/schools/Applications-for-Speech-Language-Pathology-Practice.

Bavelier, D., Green, C. S., & Dye, M. W. G. (2010). Children, wired: For better and for worse. *Neuron, 67*(5), 692-701.

Brabazon, T. (2006). *Socrates with earphones: The ipodification of education.* Centre for Critical and Cultural Studies, The University of Queensland. Retrieved June 20, 2006, from http://www.cccs.uq.edu.au/index.html?page=42950&ntemplate=365.

Chiong, C., & Shuler, C. (2010). Learning: There's an app for that? Investigations of children's usage and learning with mobile devices and apps. New York: The Joan Ganz Cooney Center at Sesame Workshop.

Department of Education and Early Childhood Development. (2010). *iPads in Special Education.* Melbourne: Communications Division for Student Wellbeing Division Department of Education and Early Childhood Development. Retrieved from www.ipadsforeducation.vic.edu.au/userfiles/files/DEECD%20iPad%20support%20booklet%20for%20special%20education.pdf.

Fernandes, B. (2010). Apps to revolutionize your therapy. *Advance Magazine, 20,* 15.

Green, J. L. (2011). *The ultimate guide to assistive technology in special education: resources for education, intervention, and rehabilitation.* Waco: Prufrock Press.

Horst, H., Herr-Stephenson, B., & Robinson, L. (2010). Media ecologies. In M. Ito, S. Baumer, M. Bittanti, d. boyd, R. Cody, B. Herr, H. A. Horst, P. G. Lange, D. Mahendran, K. Martinez, C. J. Pascoe, D. Perkel, L. Robinson, C. Sims & L. Tripp (Eds.), *Hanging out, messing around, geeking out: Living and learning with new media.* Cambridge: MIT Press.

Kelly, B., Phipps, L., & Swift, E. (2004). Developing a holistic approach for e-learning accessibility. *Canadian Journal of Learning and Technology*, 30(3). Retrieved October 13, 2006, from www.cjit.ca/content/vol30.3/kelly.html.

Marks, Genee, Milne, Jay. (2008). iPod therefore I can: Enhancing the learning of children with intellectual disabilities through emerging technologies. UB Online Repository. Retrieved September 3, 2011, from http://archimedes.ballarat.edu.au:8080/vital/access/HandleResolver/1959.17/17504.

Plowman, L., McPake, J., & Stephens, C. (2008). Just picking it up? Young children learning with technology at home. *Cambridge Journal of Education*, Vol. 38, No. 3, September 2008, 303–319.

Purcell, K., Entner, R., and Henderson, N. (2010). *The rise of apps culture*. Washington, DC: Pew Research Center's Internet and American Life Project. Downloaded September 16, 2010, from http://pewInternet.org/Reports/2010/The-Rise-of-Apps-Culture.aspx.

Shuler, C. (2007). *D is for digital: An analysis of the children's interactive media environment with a focus on mass marketed products that promote learning.* New York, NY: The Joan Ganz Cooney Center at Sesame Workshop.

Sennott, S., & Bowker, A. (2009). Autism, AAC, and Proloquo2Go. *Perspectives on Augmentative and Alternative Communication* 18:137-145.

Shuler, C. (2009a). *iLearn: A content analysis of the iTunes App Store's Education Section.* New York, NY: The Joan Ganz Cooney Center at Sesame Workshop.

Shuler, C. (2009b). *Pockets of potential: Using mobile technologies to promote children's learning.* New York, NY: The Joan Ganz Cooney Center at Sesame Workshop.

Tanenhaus, J. (February/March, 2011). Diskoveries: Apple iPad and Apps for Special Needs. *Closing the - Gap*, 29(6), 7-13.

Thai, A. M., Lowenstein, D., Ching, D., & Rejeski, D. (2009). Game changer: Investing in digital play to advance children's learning and health. New York: The Joan Ganz Cooney Center at Sesame Workshop.

Warschauer, M., & Matuchniak, T. (2010). New technology and digital worlds: Analyzing evidence of equity in access, use, and outcomes. *Review of Research in Education*, 34(179), 179-225.

Index

J

K

L

M

Magic Eyeball, 173

Magic Piano, 330

Martha Speaks Dog Party, 116

Match, 102

Math

    Jumbo Calculator, 283

    KidCalc 7-in-1 Math Fun, 276

    Math Cards, 281

    Math Flash Cards, 282

    Math Magic & Math Series, 280

    123 Animals Counting HD—for iPad, 277

    Rocket Math, 279

    Time, Money & Fractions On-Track, 278

Math Cards, 281

Math Flash Cards, 282

Math Magic & Math Series, 280

MazeFinger Plus, 246

MeMoves, 226

Micro-Expression Trainer, 170

Mini Capacitive Stylus, 366

Model Me Going Places, 152

Monkey Preschool Lunchbox, 290

Montressori Crosswords—Teach and Learn Spelling with Fun Puzzles for Children, 272

More Pizza!, 248

Motor Planning

    ActionPotato, 241

    Anaconda, 240

    Doodle Buddy—Paint, Draw, Scribble, Sketch, 237

    Fish Fingers! 3D Interactive Aquarium, 238

    Guitar Hero, 243

    Knots, 236

    Lightsaber Unleashed, 242

    MazeFinger Plus, 246

    PocketGuitar, 244

    Slide 2 Unlock, 234

    Speak Bot, 245

    Uzu, 235

    Wooly Willy, 239

Mr. Rogers Makes a Journal for Preschoolers, 127

Mr. Trivia, 162

Music, Song & Creativity

    Baby Piano, 335

    Drum Kit, 334

    Faces iMake, 331

    FingerPiano, 332

    Fun Piano, 336

    Itsy Bitsy Spider, 327

    Kids Videos and Entertainment–Kideos HD, 328

Y

Z

Stay up to date with new apps coming out by visiting *www.AutismApps.org!*

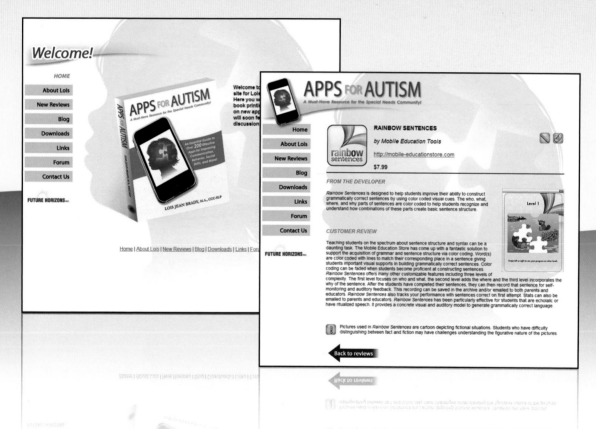

And be sure to "like" the Apps for Autism page on Facebook (www.facebook.com/AppsForAutism) so you can be in the know when long-awaited apps are released, when excellent apps are on sale (or even FREE for a limited time), and more!